Fiction and Narrative

For the past twenty years there has been a virtual consensus in philosophy that there is a special link between fiction and the imagination. In
particular, fiction has been defined in terms of the imagination: what it
is for something to be fictional is that there is some requirement that a
reader imagine it. Derek Matravers argues that this rests on a mistake; the
proffered definitions of 'the imagination' do not link it with fiction but
with representations more generally. In place of the flawed consensus,
he offers an account of what it is to read, listen to, or watch a narrative
whether that narrative is fictional or non-fictional. The view that emerges,
which draws extensively on work in psychology, downgrades the divide
between fiction and non-fiction and largely dispenses with the imagination. In the process, he casts new light on a succession of issues: on the
'paradox of fiction', on the issue of fictional narrators, on the problem of
'imaginative resistance', and on the nature of our engagement with film.

Derek Matravers is Professor of Philosophy at the Open University.

Fiction and Narrative

Derek Matravers

OXFORD
UNIVERSITY PRESS

OXFORD
UNIVERSITY PRESS

Great Clarendon Street, Oxford, OX2 6DP,
United Kingdom

Oxford University Press is a department of the University of Oxford.
It furthers the University's objective of excellence in research, scholarship,
and education by publishing worldwide. Oxford is a registered trade mark of
Oxford University Press in the UK and in certain other countries

First published 2014
First published in paperback 2017

Published in the United States of America by Oxford University Press
198 Madison Avenue, New York, NY 10016, United States of America

British Library Cataloguing in Publication Data
Data available

Library of Congress Cataloging in Publication Data
Data available

ISBN 978-0-19-964701-9 (Hbk.)
ISBN 978-0-19-877660-4 (Pbk.)

For Dom Lopes and Susan Herrington

Acknowledgements

The first draft of this book was written in the 2009/2010 academic year which I spent at the University of British Columbia in Vancouver. That I had such a fantastic time was due in part to the members of Faculty and to the support staff, but in particular to the wonderful graduate community who seemed happy to waste endless hours exploring Vancouver and environs, drinking cocktails, and talking about anything and everything including fiction and the imagination. In particular, Jill Isenberg, Joshua Johnston, and Nola Semczyszyn—thanks for everything.

It is also a pleasure to thank all my friends and colleagues who have commented on papers, or talked various issues through with me: Peter Alward, Paloma Atencia-Linares, Al Baker, Alex Barber, Chris Belshaw, Ben Blumson, Emily Caddick, Dan Came, Tim Chappell, Cristina Chimisso, Scott Clifton, David Collins, Sophia Connell, Gregory Currie, Eva Dadlez, David Davies, Stephen Davies, Fabien Dorsch, Heather Dyke, Susan Feagin, Damien Freeman, Richard Gerrig, John Holbo, Rob Hopkins, Helen Jezzard, Matthew Kieran, Justine Kingsbury, John Kulvicki, Dom Lopes, Amanda Matravers, Graham McFee, Hugh Mellor, Aaron Meskin, Daniele Moyal-Sharrock, Alex Neill, Glenn Parsons, Jon Phelan, Jon Pike, Trevor Ponech, Carolyn Price, Neil Sinhababu, Kathleen Stock, Kendall Walton, Jonathan Weinberg, and Edward Winters. Stacie Friend, whose view is broadly in the same area as mine, has been a generous friend and her book, which is due in the next few years, will take the debate in a new and exciting direction. I learned much from Peter Goldie, who died during the time in which I was revising the book, and who is much missed. Amy Coplan, who is sadly always an ocean away, has been a great help as my philosophical evil twin. I would also like to thank Madeleine Ransom who taught me more than I taught her and Alana Jelinek who I should have thanked last time. I apologize to anyone who I ought to have listed and have not; I also apologize if I have not attributed a point or argument in the text to someone where I ought to have.

I have also benefitted from some invitations to take up visiting positions in order to discuss my work, which have come along with some fabulous hospitality. In addition to all those in Vancouver, I should extend my thanks to James Maclaurin and his colleagues at Otago (and Josh Parsons for the initial invitation); Ben Blumson and his colleagues in Singapore; Glenn Parsons and his colleagues at Ryerson; and Jérôme Pelletier, Margherita Arcangeli, and colleagues in Paris. I should also thank the Open University Arts Faculty Deanery (in particular, David Rowland) for making it possible for me to take up these invitations.

Peter Momtchiloff at OUP has been his usual professional and helpful self. The three anonymous readers of the first draft provided me with some excellent advice for changes. I considered all their suggestions seriously, and almost always acted upon them. I have not acknowledged the particular points where improvements were made on the grounds of not wanting to multiply footnotes, which gives some indication of the extent to the book was improved. I am grateful to you, whoever you are.

I would also like to thank my wife, Jane Collins, for putting up with the ups and downs; you have been splendid. Thanks too to my family—and hers—for their continued interest and support.

Finally, it is a great pleasure to dedicate this book to Dom Lopes and his wife, Susan Herrington. Thanks for the invitation to Vancouver, thanks for your wonderful company and for the hospitality you showed me when I was there.

Contents

1

Introduction

Within the Anglo-American tradition there is a rich recent history of work on engaging with the written word, particularly the fictional written word.[1] More specifically, it is now over twenty years since Kendall Walton published *Mimesis as Make-Believe*, a book which shaped the debate and provided it with the concepts with which to make progress. Walton models our engagement with representations on children's games of make-believe. An example he uses is a game in which children, walking through the woods, decide that tree stumps are to count as bears. That is, a tree stump in the undergrowth mandates that the children imagine that there is a bear in the undergrowth. That there is a mandate to imagine that there is a bear in the undergrowth makes it fictional that there is a bear in the undergrowth: 'a fictional truth consists in there being a prescription or mandate in some context to imagine something' (Walton 1990). In a dazzling display of ingenuity, Walton shows how we can use this model to generate the content of fictions, to explain our psychological relations with fictional characters, to give general accounts of verbal and depictive representation (to use Walton's terms), and to explain the semantics of fictional discourse and the ontology of fictional characters.

Walton's work connects the mental state, typically a propositional attitude, of imagination (or 'make-believe') and fiction. Thus a rather nice research programme is set up. On the one side we have the actual world, beliefs, and a connection to action and on the other side we have fictional worlds, make-beliefs, and an absence of a connection to action. Investigation of the second half of this divide coincided neatly with work on the imagination in another area of philosophy: the debate between two

---

[1] Leaving aside various rich sub-fields (such as intention and interpretation and the semantics of fictional discourse) we might pick out the following prominent stepping stones: Radford 1975; Searle 1979; Currie 1990; Walton 1990.

approaches to human understanding. 'Theory theory' is the view that we understand each other by using a tacit theory and 'simulation' is the view that we understand each other by imagining what it would be like to be in the other person's situation, or to be the other person. Work on the imagination in the theory of fiction has been used to illuminate the philosophy of mind and work in the philosophy of mind has been used to illuminate our engagement with fiction.

This book bears an ambivalent relationship to Walton's magisterial achievement. While I find myself in sympathy with the broad thrust of Walton's approach, I find myself out of sympathy with much of the debate that has come thereafter. In short, I think that the debate has taken a wrong turning. There were various ways in which Walton's approach did not fit neatly together, and, over the years, these gaps have lurked below the neat surface of the literature, undermining its worth and sense. In this book I attempt to develop, and make consistent, the account of what goes on in the mind of the reader. It neglects other problems in the area; in particular, I have nothing to say about either the ontology of fictional characters or the semantics of fictional discourse. This does not imply that I think those problems are unimportant; it is only that the groundwork lies in sorting out what happens when we engage with fiction, and the ontology and semantics needs to fit around that.

I start in Chapter 2 by investigating Walton's account of fiction. Readers unfamiliar with Walton, who might not be interested in my attempt to explain why I think his view unsatisfactory, could skip this chapter as it is reasonably independent of the rest of the book. I argue that Walton has two criteria by which a proposition becomes fictional: 'the transformation criterion' and 'the engagement criterion'. I argue that although the first clearly applies to children's games of make-believe, it does not apply to fiction. I argue that the second does apply to fiction, but to a lot more besides. Hence, I conclude that Walton does not prove a connection between the imagination and fiction. I am convinced that Walton's account is much misunderstood in the literature. I am less convinced that I have fully grasped it in all its subtlety. Whether I have or not, I think the interpretation I offer is true to more of Walton's position than most.

The debate after Walton has crystallized around two points of consensus: that what it is for a proposition to be fictional is for there to be a mandate to imagine it and that the mental state of imagining a proposition can be given a functional definition that distinguishes it from believing that proposition. In Chapter 3 I argue that on the consensus definition of 'imagination' we are mandated to imagine many more propositions than those we intuitively think of as fictional. Indeed, we are mandated to imagine all propositions that are the content of representations, whether these representations are fictional or non-fictional. Imagination is not the counterpart of belief; indeed, in many cases there is no distinction between imagination and occurrent belief. Hence, the consensus view is hopeless. I provide a further positive argument against the consensus view: namely, that it is unable to deal with a self-inflicted problem—that of explaining how non-fictional and fictional propositions can work together in a seamless narrative.

Chapter 4 argues that the distinction between the non-fictional and the fictional is less fundamental than the distinction between things happening in our immediate environment and things being represented to us as happening at other times or in other places. This coincides roughly with the distinction between situations that afford the possibility of action and those that do not, but bears no relation to the distinction between non-fiction and fiction. The function of representations, I maintain, is to bring to our attention events that are not currently happening in our immediate environment. Representations could describe events that are happening at some other time or some other place, or events that might happen, could have happened, or will never happen. This puts the whole post-Waltonian debate on a different footing although, perhaps surprisingly, I do not think it is very far from Walton's own conception of the issues.

A great deal of contemporary philosophy of fiction is premised on there being a cognitive attitude peculiar to fiction. Abandoning this premise does not mean all the problems vanish, although it does mean that those that remain need to be looked at in a new light. In Chapters 5 and 6 I provide an account of our engagement with representations. Drawing extensively on the psychology of text processing, I argue that the most perspicuous account of our engaging with narratives available finds no role for the imagination. Furthermore, this account covers all narratives—whether non-fiction or fiction. I argue that engaging with a narrative is a matter of building a 'mental model' of the content of that narrative, and that the mental model is compartmentalized (although not insulated) from our pre-existing structures of belief.

If the account of engaging with narrative is neutral as to whether the narrative is non-fiction or fiction, how is that distinction to be made? The mistake made in the contemporary literature is to run together two different issues: the mechanics of our engaging with narrative and the relation between the content of those narratives and our pre-existing structures of belief. In Chapter 7 I argue that although the way we engage with narratives is the same whether they are non-fiction or fiction, there are different presuppositions as to which of the propositions that make up that content we subsequently believe. This is not to say that we believe the content of non-fictional narratives and do not believe the content of fictional narratives. The relation is a good deal more complicated. I show that although an author's Gricean intentions do not determine the manner of our engagement with a narrative, they can nonetheless help identify the beliefs we form on the grounds of such engagement. I should say here, so as not to disappoint, that I do not provide succour for anybody hoping to find a theoretical basis for downplaying the significance of the divide between truths and untruths in narratives.

It is a consequence of what I have argued so far that what we have previously taken to be problems for fiction are problems for representation more generally. In Chapter 8 I look at one specific problem: the so-called 'paradox of fiction'. I distinguish a number of different versions of this problem, and show that if there is a problem at all, it is not a problem peculiar to fiction. Indeed, one benefit of the approach I recommend is that it dissolves rather than solves some problems that have always had an air of unreality about them, of which this is a particularly prominent example.

Chapter 9 draws out three further implications of my account. First, as engaging with non-fictional and fictional representations are on a par it makes no sense for us to imagine of an instance of the latter that it is an instance of the former. That is, we need not imagine, of the fiction, that it is being related to us as known fact. Hence, we do not have *that* reason to claim that we imagine that fictional representations have narrators. All that is necessary for our engaging with a narrative is that we are engaging with information about events not currently happening in our immediate environment. It is an open question whether a narrator is invariably part of the content of our engaging with a representation, although I end up with agreeing with George Wilson and others that we need some 'minimal narrating agency'. Second, there is the problem of logically contradictory narratives. Of the several issues that arise from this, the one that interests me is the purported incompatibility of the following claims:

1. We imagine the contents of a fiction.
2. The content of some fictions are logically contradictory.
3. We cannot imagine a logical contradiction.

The appearance of incompatibility is dispelled once we realize that (3) is only true if our imagining the state of affairs is in some way full or exhaustive, yet we know that our imagining in (1) is sketchy and incomplete. It is true but harmless that there are fictions that we cannot fully or exhaustively imagine. Third, I consider one of the problems that falls under the general heading of the 'problem of imaginative resistance'. The problem that concerns me is whether we would ever be warranted in believing that false moral claims were true in a representation on the grounds of them being asserted in that representation. I argue that the structure of our engagement with representations mirrors that of testimony, and it is for this reason that the limits of what we are willing to countenance as true in a representation match the limits of what we are willing to countenance as transmissible through testimony. I have presented this view before (in Matravers 2003) and here take the opportunity to defend it against objection.

Finally, in Chapter 10, I consider, as a coda to the forgoing, what implications my view has for our engagement with film. The detailed work done on text processing enables us to see that what is going on in the head of the reader and what is going on in the head of the viewer is distinct; something hidden by the blanket claim that each is simply a case of imagining content. As our experience of film is a face-to-face experience of images, I argue that the role of the imagination is even more limited in this case than in our experience of reading. However, this chapter does not merely generalize from one medium (the written word) to another (film). It also expands on the views expressed in Chapters 3 to 6: that fiction has no special link to the imagination, and that the imagination is not needed as part of our account of engaging with representations. In particular, no special act of the imagination is needed when watching fiction films, and, furthermore, no special act of the imagination is needed to explain our engaging with films (or indeed visual representations) more generally.

If the approach taken in this book is correct there is no mental state peculiar to our engagement with fiction. Once we realize this, and get the rest of the issues into proper focus, the lie of the land changes; some problems disappear, some creases straighten out, and we have a much clearer view of the landscape as a whole.

2

Walton on Fiction

In this chapter I shall substantiate my claim, made above, that certain aspects of Walton's approach 'did not fit neatly together'. To engage with Walton's work one must take seriously his methodology of 'theory building'. He is attempting to 'construct a single comprehensive and unified theory' that explains many aspects of a vast philosophical terrain (Walton 1990: 8). There is no presupposition that the concepts currently in use are in good order; he is happy to revise or replace those that are not (Walton 2007). In *Mimesis as Make-Believe* he introduces a sharpened version of the familiar concept of the imagination ('make-believe') and uses it to bring order and system to the entire domain of the representational arts. Although the gnawing criticism of the mice may someday leave sufficient holes for it no longer to pack conviction, piecemeal criticism does not really engage with the project. This is particularly so when the criticism, in engaging with particular solutions to particular problems, is of the form that Walton violates our intuitions or distorts our concepts. Such criticisms would need to be judged against the success or failure of the theory as a whole.

As a whole, the theory is impressive. If not quite Ayer's 'solution to all outstanding philosophical disputes'[1] it does offer (to take in turn each of the four parts of the book): a general account of representation; an account of engagement with the representational arts; an account of particular forms of representation (depictive and verbal representation); and an account of the semantics and ontology of representational art. As I have said, some aspects of the account are in tension; a tension that vitiates much of the current work in the philosophy of fiction. My ambition is to present a theory that covers some of the same ground from which this tension is absent. I should say at the outset that some may think the

---

[1] The title of the final chapter of Ayer 1971.

game is not worth the candle. What emerges is a theory with less explanatory scope and—even for some explanations within its scope—some
persistent difficulties. In particular, I shall have nothing to say about the
semantic and ontological issues that arise out of our thinking about representational art. I am not sure what relation the account I present has to
semantics and ontology, although I am inclined to think that the semantics and ontology needs to follow the psychology rather than the other way
around. However, all theories need developing and, even if mine is not the
final word, I do think it takes us closer to the truth and thus provides a better alternative to that which is on offer at the moment.

Let us look, then, at the first three parts of Walton's theory. I will argue
that the claims of the first part pull against those of the second, and that
the claims of the third part can be separated (and I think rejected) without
damaging the theory as a whole. I shall leave discussion of the third part
until later in the book.

Part of Walton's project—perhaps the central part—is providing a
theoretical definition of 'the fictional'; one that will prove both illuminating and useful. He is explicit about the class of works that he wants to
delimit: they are 'works of *fiction*—novels, stories, and tales, for instance,
among literary works, rather than biographies, histories, and textbooks'
(Walton 1990: 3). Part One presents a clear criterion for the fictional. It can
be introduced by looking at Walton's helpful example of children's games
of make-believe. Walton envisages such a game in which tree stumps
count as bears. In the actual world there are tree stumps located in various
places along the walk. Once it has been stipulated that 'all tree stumps are
bears' then various things that are true in the actual world (that there is
a tree stump on Eric's right) make various things true in the game world
(that there is a bear on Eric's right). Certain games do not need explicit
stipulations. In these games, the translation from what is going on in the
actual world to what is going on in the world of the game is sanctioned
by custom and practice. Hence, in the usual games of mud pies, certain
things that are true in the actual world (that there are five globs of mud
in the cardboard box) make certain things true in the game world (that
there are five pies in the oven). To anticipate, Walton will argue that in the
same way (although a way that takes over four hundred pages fully to spell
out) the position of the paint in Seurat's *Sunday on the Island of La Grand
Jatte* makes it true in the world of the *La Grande Jatte* that there is a couple
strolling in the park; the sentences in a copy of *Gulliver's Travels* make it

true in the world of *Gulliver's Travels* that there is a society of six-inch-tall people called Lilliputians; and the sentences in Kafka's *Metamorphosis* make it true in the world of *Metamorphosis* that Gregor Samsa was transformed into an insect.

The structure of games of make-believe is as follows. A stipulation needs to be made (or understood) that will serve as a function that takes us from truths about the actual world (some proposition p) to truths within a game world (G(q)). Let us cut to the chase and allow that 'truths within the game world' are 'fictional truths' (F(q)). In other words—returning to mud pies—we need some function to take us from propositions on the left to propositions on the right.

Actual world truths	Fictional world truths
There is a glob of mud.	There is a pie.
There is a box.	There is an oven.
There are x globs of mud in the box.	There are x pies in the oven.
The globs of mud have been in the box for y minutes.	The pies have been in the oven for y minutes.

Those propositions on the left are true in the actual world. Given the game, it is the fact that each is true in the actual world that makes the corresponding proposition on the right true in the fictional world.

If one stands back, there is something very attractive about this. The world of the arts is full of things that have one identity in the actual world and another identity in the world of the arts. There are paint-smeared canvases that are views of parks; there are cheap paperbacks that are eighteenth-century sailor's journals; there are strings of sound that are expressions of emotion; there are carved stones that are the figures of minutemen. The list could go on. If Walton can provide a theory that can, systematically, take us from something that has one identity in the actual world to another identity in the fictional world (or more generally, the world of the arts) it would have powerful explanatory weight.

So far all we need is a function to take us from something in the actual world to something else in the fictional world. To quote Walton, 'The stump in the thicket makes it fictional that a bear is there only because there is a certain convention understanding, agreement in the game of make-believe, one to the effect that wherever there is a stump there is a bear' (Walton 1990: 38). For all that I have said, that function could simply be a matter of making the right stipulations: if p, then F(q); if r, then F(s). However, this is not Walton's view. For Walton, what takes us from the truths of the actual world to the truths of the world of fictions is *a prescription to imagine*. The stipulations (or understandings) of a game of make-believe are really prescriptions to imagine. Once it is stipulated that all tree stumps are bears, those playing the game are prescribed to imagine a whole raft of propositions: that there are bears around, that there is a bear in that thicket, that there is a bear to the right of Eric and so on. On encountering a tree stump, they are prescribed to imagine encountering a bear. Let us introduce some Waltonian terminology. What I have so far been calling 'stipulations' are a special case of what he calls *principles of generation*. A *fictional truth* 'consists in there being a prescription or mandate in some context to imagine something' (Walton 1990: 39). A *prop* is something that mandates imaginings, hence 'Props are generators of fictional truths, things which, by virtue of their nature or existence, make propositions fictional (Walton 1990: 37). Finally, something is an *object* of imagining if we are prescribed to imagine something of that very thing. Hence, the tree stump is not only a prop (it prescribes that it be imagined that there is a bear) it is also an object of imagining (the prescription is that we imagine, of that very tree stump, that it is a bear). Walton summarizes his view as follows (I have included some claims not yet discussed for completeness):

> *Representations*, I have said, are things possessing the social function of serving as props in games of make-believe, although they also prompt imaginings and are also *objects* of them as well. A prop is something which, by virtue of conditional *principles of generation*, mandates imaginings. Propositions whose imaginings are mandated are *fictional*, and the fact that a given proposition is fictional is a *fictional truth*. *Fictional worlds* are associated with collections of fictional truths; what is fictional is fictional in a given world—the world of a game of make-believe for example, or that of a representational work of art. (Walton 1990: 69)

I have not spelled out all of Walton's careful considerations in favour of his account. This is because, provisionally, I am going to accept his position. My worry is not (yet) with the details of the argument, but with pointing out that there are two claims being made here. The first claim underpinning the general theory is that some function will take us from truths in the actual world to truths in the fictional world and the second claim is that this function is a prescription to imagine. Why a prescription to imagine? Why not, as looked possible, simply do it in terms of stipulated (or understood) principles of generation? My argument will be that Walton provides good reasons to invoke prescriptions to imagine. However, the cost is that he no longer has a simple divide between actual worlds and fictional worlds. Indeed, the category of the fictional eventually has to drop out altogether. Then, perhaps surprisingly, so does the imagination.

Why, then, does Walton invoke the imagination as the mechanism to take us from actual world truths to fictional world truths? After all, he explicitly allows that the imagination is not necessary in order to grasp fictional truths. Someone could, without using their imagination, 'take a great interest in the game ... study it and its props thoroughly, learning what is fictional, which fictional truths imply which others, what principles of generation are operative' (Walton 1990: 209). To be more accurate, this is possible for some games; it is not possible for engaging with pictures—or, as Walton calls them, 'depictive representations'. Let us put pictures to one side (in fact, I shall largely put them to one side until the final chapter of the book) and return to children's games of make-believe and whether the lessons learned there can be transferred to our engaging with the written word or, as Walton calls them, 'verbal representations'.

The reason Walton evokes the imagination is that only it can explain our psychological engagement with fictions. I shall group such engagements under two headings: perspective and vivacity. Let us consider perspective first. In the game of make-believe in which tree stumps are to count for bears, the game is played best when the participants do not merely imagine things of tree stumps but also things of themselves. Instead of merely imagining, on turning the corner and finding a tree stump, of the tree stump that it is a bear, Eric imagines of himself that he is confronted by a bear. Walton calls this 'imagining from the inside'.

> Imagining from the inside is one variety of what I will call 'imagining *de se*,' a form of self-imagining characteristically described as imagining *doing* or *experiencing* something (or *being* a certain way), as opposed to merely *that* one does or experiences a certain property. (Walton 1990: 29)

Let us grant (as it is true) that, in their games of make-believe, children do not simply cognize lists of fictional truths. Instead, their mental states are roughly as Walton describes. Such a mental state seems straightforwardly one of imagination. It is difficult to see how we could describe Eric's situation as anything but him imagining of himself that he is confronted by a bear.

Walton does not say very much about vivacity. Putting aside what he says about our engaging with depictive representations, it is seldom mentioned in the book. However, when it is mentioned what Walton says is interesting. The core of the argument is laid out in a discussion of spontaneous versus deliberate imaginings. Once again, the example is the game in which stumps count for bears.

> If Jennifer imagines herself coming across a bear in a forest, she has bearish thoughts; she entertains, considers, turns over in her mind the proposition that there is a bear in front of her, and probably more specific propositions as well, such as that there is a ferocious grizzly pacing back and forth in front of her. She may also visualize a bear. If her imagining is deliberate, the fact that she rather than a (real) bear is the source of these bearish thoughts and images, the fact that she dreamed up the bear, is sure to be prominent in her awareness and difficult to ignore. It is not so difficult to ignore this if her imagining is spontaneous. She *knows* perfectly well that no real bear is responsible for her thoughts and images; she may have no doubt that they flow from somewhere in the dark recesses of her own unconscious. But when her imagining is spontaneous, nothing forces her to dwell on this fact; it does not intrude into her occurrent thoughts, even though if asked she would not hesitate to acknowledge it. This is why the imagining is likely to be more vivid, more gripping, more 'frightening' if it is spontaneous than if it is deliberate. (Walton 1990: 15)

In using the imagination, we open the door to affective experiences. The nature of the affect will depend upon the content of what is imagined, and the force of the affect will depend (amongst other things) on whether the imagining is deliberate or spontaneous and whether or not there is an object of our imaginings. The affect tends to be more forceful when there is an object than when there is not ('they provide "substance" to one's imaginings, thereby enhancing their "vivacity"' (Walton 1990: 116)). Walton confirms his view later in the book: 'if one imagines [a proposition] with minimal vivacity, one is unlikely to have the experience of fictionally being concerned or upset or relieved or frightened or overjoyed by the fact that it is true' (Walton 1990: 274).

There is an omission in Walton's argument here that might strike some as curious. Why did he not take the obvious route of giving an account of the imagination and showing it to be the attitude to propositions that are fictionally true in the way that belief is the attitude to propositions that are actually true? We have some pro-attitude to propositions such as 'Sherlock Holmes is a detective' which is not belief but which shares some of the properties of belief. Why not argue directly for the existence of this attitude? Indeed, this—as we shall see in the next chapter—is the approach taken by many who have come after Walton. Here I sympathize with Walton's caution; he seems to me right to take this option. After eight pages of carefully discriminating various aspects of the imagination he throws up his hands at providing a definition, concluding instead that ' "Imagining" can, if nothing else, serve as a placeholder for a notion yet to be fully clarified' (Walton 1990: 21).

So far, I have described the argument of the first two parts of Walton's book with respect to children's games of make-believe; now let us apply the lessons of these arguments to verbal representations. There are a number of problems that arise. The first lies in imagination's role in transforming a proposition in the actual world into a different proposition in the fictional world. I shall call the claim that something is a fiction if the imagination is required to transform a proposition in the actual world into a different proposition in the fictional world 'the transformation criterion'. Here is a passage from *Mimesis as Make-Believe* where Walton appears to be using this criterion.

It is reasonably obvious, often enough, that a passage in a novel is to be construed as a more or less straightforward observation or pronouncement about the actual world, addressed by the author directly to the readers. The opening sentence of *Anna Karenina* ('Happy families are all alike; every unhappy family is unhappy in its own way') is frequently cited; there are discussion of love and other matters of real-world interest in Henry Fielding's novels; in footnotes to *Kiss of the Spider Woman* Manuel Puig presents a series of apparently straightforward essays recounting the views of Freud, Norman O. Brown, Herbert Marcuse, Wilhelm Reich, and others on sexuality. But it is rarely wholly clear that such passages do not also have the function of eliciting imaginings, of making it fictional, for instance, that someone—a character through whom the author speaks or even the author himself—is making those pronouncements. If, in setting down the opening lines of *Anna Karenina*, Tolstoy was claiming (with allowance for some exaggeration) that all happy families really are alike but that there are many different kinds of unhappy ones, his words may also make it fictional that someone—the narrator—utters them assertively. If this is their function, the passage is fiction in our sense. (Walton 1990: 90–91)

Walton allows that some passages of novels can be construed as non-fictional: 'more or less straightforward observation or pronouncement about the actual world'. However, with others, the pronouncement

changes its identity: an 'un-owned' claim in the actual world is transformed into—for example—someone's utterance in the fictional world. If
there is such a change the passage is fictional; if there is not such a change,
the passage is not fictional.

For the principal example of the transformation criterion, however, we
have to look at depictive representations. Walton holds the initially rather
surprising view that 'pictures are fictional by definition' (Walton 1990: 351).
This is surprising as one might think that the distinction between fictions
and non-fictions, between pictures of Superman and courtroom sketches
for example, is the same as can be found in the case of verbal representations. Walton is committed to his view, however, as in all cases of depictive
representation the state of affairs in the actual world makes true some different state of affairs in the fictional world. By the transformation criterion this makes all cases of depictive representation fictional. In the actual
world a person looks at a flat piece of canvas covered with pigment, which
makes it the case in the fictional world that a person looks (say) at a mill. In
Walton's words, 'one imagines of one's seeing of the canvas to be a seeing of
a mill' (Walton 1990: 301).

The problem with the transformation criterion is that it appears not
to be true of many verbal representations that we take to be fictional. In
the Raymond Chandler's novel, *The Little Sister*, the following sentence
occurs: 'Room 332 was at the back of the building, near the door to the fire
escape' (Chandler 1955: 48). In the actual world, this sentence expresses
a proposition and the very same proposition is the one that is true in the
fictional world. As there is no transformation, the transformation criterion (the claim that something is a fiction if the imagination is required
to transform a proposition in the actual world into a different proposition
in the fictional world) will not distinguish actual propositions from fiction propositions. All that I need to read and understand that sentence is
a grasp of English. It is true that we will need an account of what it is for
that sentence to be fictional; my point at the moment is only that it is nothing to do with the kinds of transformations characteristic of the kinds of
games of make-believe to which Walton claims fictions are analogous.

Walton is well aware of this, of course, and has two replies. The first,
which was evident in the quotation above, is to claim that there is a
transformation. The proposition true in the fictional world *is* different: perhaps in the fictional world the sentence is uttered by Marlowe or
perhaps by some other narrator. The second is to accept that there is no

transformation; as Walton puts it 'Some literary works might be thought of in just this way, as simply mandating the imagining of the propositions their sentences specify' (Walton 1990: 353). Neither of these replies seems to me satisfactory.

The first is not satisfactory because the standard case is that there is no transformation. All that is required to follow a fictional verbal representation is a grasp of the language in which it is written (let us assume it is in English). One might try to argue that there will always be some transformation because, at a minimum, in the actual world the proposition is false and in the fictional world the proposition is true. Versions of this claim (which is surprisingly tenacious) will appear throughout the book so I will simply make two points against it here. First, this is not a change in the content of the proposition. It is not analogous to 'there is a tree stump in the thicket' being transformed into 'there is a bear in the thicket'. Second, it is difficult to see what the additional step adds. I read *The Little Sister*, fully aware that it is fictional, and, being a competent reader of English, I grasp its content. In some perfectly clear and innocuous sense, we can hold that the content is 'true in the fiction'. I cannot see that this says more than that the proposition is fictional. Furthermore, I cannot see what could be gained by the claim that we imagine it is true—how could such an endeavour on our part possibly give us anything we do not have already? Walton's second reply is not satisfactory as a defence of the transformation thesis as it amounts to simply giving up the thesis.

Walton might want to defend the transformation thesis on more general grounds. As he says 'that make-believe (or imagination, or pretense) of some sort is central, somehow, to works of fiction is surely beyond question' (Walton 1990: 4). I have conceded—for current purposes—that in some cases of verbal representation and all cases of depictive representation there is a transformation. If the transformation criterion operates so that some propositions count as fictional, why not use this as a basis for arguing that related propositions are also fictional? Being fictional, we are mandated to imagine them. Although redundant, it does not look as if there is anything wrong with imagining exactly those propositions specified in whatever one is reading. This may look objectionable on the grounds that the transformation criterion was supposed to *determine* what was fictional, and hence *determine* what propositions we are mandated to imagine. Now it looks as if we need to know which propositions are fictional in order to know which to imagine. However, one can see ways around that. One might have other ways of specifying that a work is fictional, or perhaps we could say that if the transformation criterion is true of some large proportion of the propositions specified in a work, we can take that as a mandate to imagine the propositions that do not conform to the criterion. In that way, the essential link between fiction and the imagination is preserved.

I would reject this defence on two grounds. I am not impressed by the claim that make-believe is central to works of fiction—at least, the technical sense of 'make-believe' developed by Walton and those who have come after him. However, the main point is that I do not think that the transformation thesis is central to fictional verbal representations in the way that it is central to children's games of make-believe. The tree stump is transformed into a bear, but the propositions in a verbal representation are not standardly transformed into anything. They remain the propositions that they always have been.

Having discussed the transformation criterion, let us move on to the claim that something is fictional if it engages our imagination as only the imagination can account for facts concerning our engagement with fiction. I shall call this 'the engagement criterion'. Once again, I shall focus on verbal representations, bringing depictive representations in only when I need to in order to make a point. The claim, to remind ourselves, is that certain representations mandate us to imagine the propositions specified in them so that we can adopt a certain perspective (typically a first personal perspective) and also engage with the content with a degree of vivacity. Such representations are fictional representations.

The clear problem with this is that the range of representations that mandate us to imagine the propositions specified in them is a great deal wider than the traditional category of fiction. Consider perspective: the claim that sometimes we are mandated to imagine not merely that something is true, but to imagine doing or experiencing something. Instead of imagining that Emma has gone out in her carriage, we are mandated to imagine seeing Emma go out in her carriage. Imagining from the inside is probably an unusual part of our engagement with verbal depictions; in reading a text we are not usually mandated to do or experience something. However, the question is whether, in as much as it does occur, it occurs only when we read fiction. The answer is obvious. In as much as verbal representations mandate *de se* imaginings, they will do so whether they are fiction or non-fiction. If a passage from *Madame Bovary* can mandate that I imagine seeing Emma, a passage from my biography of Churchill can mandate that I imagine seeing the House of Commons provoke Chamberlain's resignation. Any reasons in favour of the first will count equally as reasons in favour of the second. It is, if anything, even more obvious that vivacity is not characteristic only of our engagement with fiction; there is no reason to think that the mental states provoked by fictional verbal representations are, generally, any more or less vivid than those provoked by non-fictional verbal representations.

The point has been made by another of Walton's commentators:

…any works of history, biography, and autobiography, newspaper articles, journal entries, and so forth, insofar as they aim in any of their features to prescribe imaginings, will count as fiction for Walton. Yet, numerous works of history are designed to get the reader to imagine, say, what it was like to live in a different time and place, and most interesting works have this as at least one of their goals. (Friend 2008: 153)

There are two places in *Mimesis as Make-Believe* where Walton appears to concede this. First, in discussing 'the New Journalism' he admits that 'the New Journalist, like journalists of old, can probably be construed as asserting what he writes'. Nonetheless, faced with a sample of their work (he quotes a passage from Norman Mailer's *The Executioner's Song*) there is 'no doubt that it, no less than most novels, has the function of prescribing imaginings' (Walton 1990: 80). This is, arguably, a case of a representation that passes the engagement criterion that is not fiction. Second, Walton allows that some historical representations pass the criterion:

Some histories are written in such a vivid, novelistic style that they almost inevitably induce the reader to imagine what is said, regardless of whether or not he believes it. (Indeed this may be true of Prescott's *History of the Conquest of Peru*.) If we think of the work as prescribing such a reaction, it serves as a prop in a game of make-believe. (Walton 1990: 71)

Walton has picked his examples carefully. In the first case, Mailer describes certain mental states and reports certain conversations about which he cannot possibly have known. Similarly, the propositions specified in Prescott's *History* reach beyond an historian's sober epistemological grasp. These are not clear counterexamples to the engagement criterion even by the traditional conception of fiction.

Although his careful choice of examples leaves him innocent of inconsistency, I cannot see how Walton can prevent a wholesale swamping of his category of fiction. Walton's official position is liberal. He claims that 'any work with the function of serving as a prop in a game of make-believe, *however minor or peripheral or instrumental this function might be*, qualifies as "fiction"' (italics my own) (Walton 1990: 72). The problem is that, shorn of the support of the transformation criterion, pretty much any narrative representations will mandate us to use our imagination. We can agree with Walton that (some) newspaper articles, instruction manuals, and geography textbooks, together with many or most books on science, technology and engineering, recipe books, and the like do not require that we use our imagination. The reason for this (as we shall see) is that they are not narratives. However, histories and biographies *are* narratives. This includes one of Walton's examples of non-fiction, Sandburg's biography of Lincoln, which notoriously subordinates historical detail to broader imaginative sweep.

Walton's examples suggest that he was relying on the transformation criterion to prevent the deluge Friend describes. However, as we have seen, the transformation criterion does not help. Although Walton works hard to avoid being tripped up by the tensions I have been describing, they are manifest in full force in two places in the book: in his discussion of depictive representations and his discussion of psychological participation. Once we have sorted out the arguments there, it becomes clear that for Walton the significant distinction is not between non-fictions and fictions, but between (roughly) face-to-face encounters and representations (whether non-fictional or fictional).

Above we saw that Walton's account of depictive representation commits him to the claim that all pictures are subject to the transformation criterion. The relevant issue here is that, because he thinks that transformation requires the imagination, all pictures mandate the use of our imaginations. Hence, as we have seen, all pictures are fictions. This is so regardless of their content: a picture is fiction merely in virtue of being a depictive representation. Hence, with respect to depictive representations, Walton is ready to override the traditional distinction between non-fiction and fiction. The relevant divide here is between face-to-face encounters and depictive representations.

Walton motivates his discussion of psychological participation with the example of affective involvement with fictions. These can take the form of affective states seemingly felt for ourselves, such as feeling threatened by a predatory slime apparently heading towards us from the cinema screen, or affective states felt for another, such as (to take the standard example) pity directed at Anna Karenina. What could the problem be here? Such states are familiar, and provoke no obvious puzzlement. The puzzle, Walton says, lies in the absence of any link between the emotion and action:

> We feel a psychological bond towards fictions, and intimacy with them, of a kind we ordinarily feel only toward things we take to be actual, things that are not (or are not thought to be) isolated physically from us. To allow that mere fictions are objects of our psychological attitudes while disallowing the possibility of physical interaction severs the normal links between the physical and the psychological. What is pity or anger which is never to be acted on? What is love that cannot be expressed to its object and is logically or metaphysically incapable of consummation? We cannot even try to rescue Robinson Crusoe from his island, no matter how deep our concern for him. (Walton 1990: 196)

I shall give a full, and largely sympathetic, discussion of Walton's view in Chapter 7. The point here is that Walton takes the problematic cases to be those in which our emotion is directed towards an object and any action that would usually follow from such an emotion is impossible. Walton argues that his overall theory can explain away the puzzlement. In brief, such 'emotions' take place in a structure of prescriptions to imagine—that is, within games of make-believe.

The tension is now evident. Walton's criterion picks out cases as problematic if there is no possibility of our acting on an emotion we feel towards someone or something. It is such cases that mandate imagining. However, there is no possibility of our acting on an emotion we feel towards someone or something in many non-fictional representations. It is true that we cannot even try to rescue Robinson Crusoe, but neither can we try to rescue Alexander Selkirk (the actual castaway on which the fiction of Robinson Crusoe was based). It matters not one wit whether we are reading *Robinson Crusoe* or Richard Steele's documentary account of Selkirk's time as a castaway. Representations generally depict events that are taking place outside of the sphere of our possible action either because they are removed in time (all histories) or in place (reports from elsewhere). Walton is not capturing the traditional category of fiction, he is also capturing representations traditionally thought of as non-fiction.

My claim has been that Walton's assimilation of fiction to make-believe asks us to think about the former in two different ways: of the actual world making something the case in the fictional world, and in mandating the imagination. I have argued that, at least with respect to verbal representations, the first does not hold (I will argue for a similar conclusion with respect to depictive representations in Chapter 10). The second does not pick out anything like the traditional class of fictions, but representations more generally. In short, there is nothing that I have considered so far to persuade us that there is any special link between fiction (as traditionally construed) and the imagination.

3
Fiction and the Imagination

We can divide Walton's view as to what it takes for something to be a fictional truth into two claims. The first is that there is a prescription that we imagine it: 'A fictional truth consists in there being a prescription or mandate in some context to imagine something' (Walton 1990: 39). The second is that prescription emerges as a result of various 'principles of generation'. There appears to be a consensus amongst philosophers of fiction on the first part.[1] There is less of a consensus on the second part, although one popular option is a Gricean approach. That is, authors indulge in an act of 'fiction-making' where, to quote Gregory Currie, 'the author intends that we make-believe the text (or rather its constituent propositions) and he intends to get us to do this by means of our recognition of that very intention' (Currie 1990: 30). The second claim would only be a concern if the first claim were true. As my argument is that the first claim is not true, the second claim need not concern me. That is, I shall argue against there being a necessary connection between a proposition being fictional and there being a prescription (of any sort) that we imagine it. That is, I shall argue that the following claim is false:

> FI: What it is to be fictional that p (F(p)) is for there to be a prescription that we imagine that p.

In an as-yet unpublished paper Walton himself attacks FI. The counter-examples he brings forward against the claim include a photograph taken at the moment that a golf ball passes the face of a spectator. The timing has worked out such that, humorously, it looks as if the spectator has a white spherical nose. That is, understanding the point of the photograph

---

[1] See Currie 1990: 31; Lamarque and Olsen 1994: 45–6; Carroll 1997: 205; Meskin and Weinberg 2006; Davies 2007: 32–48; Stock 2011 to take only a selection. In what follows, when I discuss the view, I will cite only the philosopher (if any) I am quoting.

requires imagining of the image of the golf ball that it is the image of the spectator's nose. However, it is not fictional in the photograph that the spectator has a golf ball for a nose. My argument is not along these lines and hence I shall ignore this wrinkle in the debate.

I shall begin by distinguishing two problems, the relation between which is the subject of much debate (although in general the consensus view considers both together). The first is the issue of what goes on in the mind of the reader of a story. Walton says that 'Imagining (propositional imagining), like (propositional) believing or desiring, is *doing* something *with* a proposition one has in mind' (Walton 1990: 20). My first problem is what, when are imagining, we *are* doing with a proposition. That is, it is an issue of what is going on in the reader's head.

The second is the classificatory problem of what makes a proposition or a work fictional. One answer to this is that a proposition is fictional if there is a mandate to imagine it, and a work is fictional if it consists of fictional propositions. As we shall see, such an answer suffers from a number of defects. For the moment, however, I simply want to distinguish the issue of the nature of the mental state (imagining that p) from the issue of the classification of the proposition or work (is it fictional that p). We can grasp the difference between these two if we look at Gregory Currie's attempt to define 'fiction'.

As we have seen, Currie takes a proposition to be fictional if its author intends that we imagine it, and intends that he gets us to do this by recognition of this very intention. In the spirit of the last chapter, one might think there are countless counterexamples to this. If it is the case that what it is to engage with a representation is to imagine its content, then, by Currie's definition, 'the fictional' will include all representations. However, this is not the counterexample Currie considers. Instead, he proposes the following.

Smith has real-life experiences of so horrible a kind that he represses them. He then invents, so he supposes, a story, and this story exactly retells these events. This is no coincidence; Smith's subconscious somehow provides him with the information for his story. (Currie 1990: 45)

In this case there is an intention that the reader should imagine the propositions that make up the story, yet the story is not fiction. Currie's solution is to add a further condition: that 'if the work is true, then it is at most accidentally true' (Currie 1990: 46). This nicely reveals the difference between the two problems. The first is the one talked about in the quotation from Walton: what is going on in the head of the reader. What is it that the reader is supposed to *do* with the propositions? The second is the question of the correct way to classify the story: is it fiction or is it non-fiction? Currie's second clause in definition addresses the second question. That is, the correct classification of the work depends in part on the genesis of the story. However, the second clause is independent of the answer we give to the first question. Facts about the genesis of the story will not illuminate the nature of the mental state of propositional imagining.

I am not sure whether Currie thinks that the readers of Smith's story should or should not imagine it. To anticipate, neither answer seems to fit easily into his overall account. As we shall see, Currie thinks we believe rather than imagine non-fictional propositions, which suggests he thinks readers should not imagine Smith's story but believe it. However, the example holds that Smith does not know his story is apt for belief, and so we can assume his readers to not either. Hence, they should imagine it. Rather than being a problem, one might hold that the independence of Currie's two criteria is a strength of the theory. After all, it is not the case that readers are stymied; they are able to engage with Smith's story whatever the facts about its genesis. This comes at a price for Currie, however, for now it looks as if what goes on in the reader's head (what they *do* with a proposition) is independent of the facts of whether the story is fictional or non-fictional.

I shall just make a quick aside about the classification problem before returning to my main theme. Even if we grant Currie's solution, he still faces the problem that many fictional works contain propositions that are non-accidentally true and which we are intended to believe (an example would be the details of the French invasion of Russia in *War and Peace*). He bites the bullet, and accepts that a work of fiction is 'a patchwork of truth and falsity, reliability and unreliability, fiction-making and assertion' (Currie 1990: 49). An alternative solution has been suggested by David Davies who appeals to the notion of a 'fidelity constraint': someone follows this constraint if they include 'only the events she believes to have occurred, narrated as occurring in the order in which she believes them to have occurred' (Davies 2007: 46). My view does not escape the classification problem, although it does throw it into slightly different relief. However, it will be a while until I return to this (towards the end of Chapter 7).

Putting that issue to one side, let us consider the first problem: what goes on in the head of the reader of a story. The consensus view holds that what goes on in reading non-fiction differs from what goes on in reading fiction and that the difference is to do with the difference between belief and imagination. I shall argue that, taken on its own terms, the consensus view is wrong about this difference. An accurate account of the difference solves some problems and changes the nature of others. So far I have taken the consensus to be adherence to FI. However, at least according to Timothy Schroeder and Carl Matheson, there is also a consensus on the nature of the imagination. Schroeder and Matheson claim that there is 'a convergence, and a certain amount of agreement upon the existence of such a convergence' about the mental attitude taken towards fictions. This is a 'distinctive cognitive attitude' ('DCA'): 'a DCA activated by fictions—not belief, but not entirely unlike belief' (Schroeder and Matheson 2006: 21). Their paper goes on to explore the properties of these DCAs with the particular purpose of showing how they can explain the relation between imagining certain states of affairs and the arousal of emotions. Schroeder and Matheson characterize the 'DCA' as follows.

Evidence that a DCA mediates between the imagination and our feelings needs to show three things: (1) that imagining that p characteristically involves or provokes the forming of a content-bearing mental state with the content p; (2) that these mental states are strongly differentiated from beliefs and perceptions (etc.) in their functional roles, thus counting as distinct attitudes; and (3) that these mental states produce the feelings we associate with emotionally laden imaginative acts. (Schroeder and Matheson 2006: 24)

I shall simply grant (1). Whatever our attitude to the content of fiction, it is going to be some 'content-bearing mental state'. My interest lies in claim (2). I shall discuss (3)—or what remains of (3)—in Chapters 5 and 8.

Schroeder and Matheson claim that the view that the imagination (or a 'DCA') can be distinguished from belief by virtue of their functional roles is a near consensus in the philosophy of fiction. They cite the following philosophers as part of the consensus: Noel Carroll, Gregory Currie, Ian Ravenscroft, Susan Feagin, Peter McComick, Aaron Meskin and Jonathan Weinberg, Roger Scruton, Kendall Walton, Sarah Worth, and Robert Yanal. It is a mistake to include Walton on this list as he is explicitly sceptical of this approach: 'It is not easy to see what behavioural criteria might throw light on imagining, or what the relevant functions of a functional account might be' (Walton 1990: 20). However, the omission of Walton is more than made up for by the addition of others who have contributed to the debate since Schroeder and Matheson's paper was written. These include David Davies, Kathleen Stock, and the authors of the other papers in the volume in which Schroder and Matheson's paper appeared (Nichols 2006; Davies 2007; Stock 2011).

My argument is simple: the consensus view's own definition of the imagination establishes no particular link to fiction. To show that the consensus view lacks foundation I shall examine its most developed account of imagination: that of Currie (and Currie and Ravenscroft). As this view is amenable to several different interpretations this will need to be done at some length. I shall then consider the views of Meskin and Weinberg.

Currie presents his views in a number of places. I shall consider two: his 1995 book, *Image and Mind*, and his 2002 book (written with Ian Ravenscroft), *Recreative Minds*. In *Image and Mind* Currie identifies imagination with simulation. He says that 'the imagination is simulation' and later that what he has provided is 'an assimilation of imagination with simulation' (Currie 1995: 151, 161). Simulation is a matter of projecting ourselves into another situation.

To imagine having those beliefs and desires is to take on, temporarily, those beliefs and desires; they become, temporarily and with other qualifications I shall describe in a moment, my own beliefs and desires. Being, thus temporarily, my own, they work their own effects on my mental economy, having the sorts of impacts on how I feel and what I decide to do that my ordinary, real beliefs and desires have. I let my mental processes run as if I really were in that situation—except that those processes run 'off-line,' disconnected from their normal sensory inputs and behavioural outputs. (Currie 1995: 144)

The key to this is that the mental states are run 'off line'; they are severed from their usual inputs and also from their usual outputs. Currie gives an example that is worth quoting at length.

For example, I might start off my imagining by taking on in this way the beliefs and desires, and also the perceptions, of someone who sees a lion rushing towards him. These beliefs and desires then operate on me through their own natural powers; I start (if my imagining is vivid enough) to feel the visceral sensations of fear, and I decide to flee. But I don't flee; these beliefs and desires—let us call them pretend or imaginary beliefs and desires—differ from my own real beliefs and desires not just in being temporary and cancellable. Unlike my real beliefs and desires, they are run off-line, disconnected from the normal perceptual inputs and behavioural outputs. I start my simulation without actually seeing a lion, and end it at the point where the decision is made, but before that decision is translated into action. The function of the simulation is not to save me from a lion, since I am not actually threatened by one, but to help me understand the mental processes of someone so threatened. (Currie 1995: 144–5)

There are three important respects in which a simulated state differs from a non-simulated state: the input, the nature of the mental states, and the output. I shall consider these in reverse order.

The output is perhaps the simplest. Currie repeatedly makes it clear that a simulation is disconnected from the normal behavioural outputs. The result of a simulation is not an action but a better understanding of 'the mental processes of someone so threatened'. Notice that Currie nowhere makes the false claim that simulation cannot result in action. To show why this is false, let me introduce some terminology (this will be rather rough for the moment, it will be sharpened later). Let us call the scenario that is simulated (being attacked by a lion) the 'simulated scenario' and the focus of the simulation (the lion) the 'simulated object'. The simulation does not cause me to act within the simulated scenario or away from or towards the simulated object for the very good reason that, as Currie says, 'I am not actually threatened by [it]'. However, there is no reason why the simulation cannot result in action outside the simulated scenario. Now that I understand what it is like to be threatened by a lion I take great care to avoid lions, I check the anti-lion fencing on my property, and so on and so forth. Indeed, as simulation is a general account of how we understand each other, and as one purpose of understanding each other is to co-ordinate action, simulation generally does result in action (only not action in the simulated scenario).

Next we have the mental states themselves. Let us consider the belief that I am being attacked by a lion and the desire not to be mauled by the lion. As Currie says, these are not 'my real beliefs and desires'. In the circumstance Currie describes, the desire (not to be mauled by a lion) will be one I already possess (although we are able to simulate desires that we do not already possess). Let us focus instead on the belief. In this circumstance, the belief ('*I* am being attacked by a lion') is false. It is important, however, that we distinguish two sorts of case. The first is when I simulate a completely hypothetical situation; I am not putting myself in any particular person's shoes. In this case the content of the belief describes no actual situation. The second is when I simulate an actual situation; I do put myself in some particular person's shoes and simulate something that actually happened (or is actually happening) to that person. In this case, the contents of my beliefs do describe some actual situation—only a situation that is not happening to me, now. Once again, as simulation is a general account of how we understand each other, the scenarios we simulate will often (if not generally) be actual. As Currie says, we have this ability so that we can put ourselves in others' situations in order to understand them.

Finally, we have the input. Currie claims that simulations are 'disconnected from their normal perceptual inputs'. In the example he gives us, the input is an imagined perception (we imagine seeing a lion rush towards us). Putting the point generally, the input to a simulated scenario is not a perception of that scenario (and, in particular, not a perception of the simulated object).

Simulation (or as Currie later calls it, 'perspective shifting') has no special link with fiction. A simulated scenario is simply one which does not have a perception of that scenario as an input and which does not have an action in that scenario as an output (Currie 1995: 150). Putting the point another way, our mental states are run off line when (roughly) they are part of some scenario we entertain that is not caused by, or has as objects, things in our egocentric space.

The difference between Currie's view and my own is not to do with his claim that 'we do not acquire from [fiction] beliefs in the straightforward way that we acquire beliefs from non-fiction'. What we are investigating is what we are doing when, in Walton's words, we are 'doing something' with a proposition. My objection to Currie is that his functional characterization of this activity—non-standard inputs and an absence of motivation as an output—does not apply only to fiction but to our engaging with representations generally. There is a further question of the relation between this activity and our pre-existing structures of belief. That is not to do with engaging in simulation, but with the *result* of engaging in simulation. Put very roughly, simulating fiction scenarios does not result in our forming beliefs and simulating non-fictional scenarios does result in our forming beliefs. I shall provide a more accurate account of this difference in Chapter 7, but we can put it to one side for the moment.

I shall look at two passages in which Currie draws a contrast between engaging with fiction and engaging with non-fiction.

Consider first a nonfictional work: a newspaper article or television documentary. If we think the work reliable, we shall form certain beliefs based on the information the work conveys. We may also acquire certain desires: documentaries about the dangers of smoking can make you want to give up, and travel articles extolling the virtues of an exotic location can make you want to go there. (So as to simplify things, I will concentrate on the case of belief for the moment.)

A fictional work, assuming we know that it's fiction, can have effects on our mental processes similar in various ways to the effects of nonfiction. Fictional works can engage our attention, and they can have what is, on reflection, a surprising capacity to move us. But we do not acquire from them beliefs in the straightforward way that we acquire beliefs from nonfiction. With fictions, our mental processes are engaged off-line, and what we acquire instead of beliefs is *imaginings* which simulate belief. (Currie 1995: 148)

In this passage Currie contrasts our engaging with non-fiction and our engaging with fiction, characterizing the first in terms of belief and the second in terms of the imagination. It is unclear how this corresponds to the difference between being attacked by a lion and simulating being attacked by a lion. In neither case is the input a perception of the simulated scenario or the output action in that scenario. Currie might respond that engaging with non-fiction is not simulation because it does result in action: 'documentaries about the dangers of smoking can make you want to give up, and travel articles extolling the virtues of an exotic location can make you want to go there'. However, as we have seen, actions of this sort are characteristic of simulations. The actions which are ruled out are those towards objects in the egocentric space of the person doing the simulation (for the obvious reason that the simulated object is not in our egocentric space) and in this respect there is no contrast between the two situations. The desire to give up smoking could be caused by a gruelling medical drama and the desire to travel to exotic places by a fiction film set in India. Non-fictional and fictional narratives do not differ systematically in their capacity to cause actions by the indirect means of causing desires.

The second passage follows immediately after the first.

When I work out what Sally believes about the location of her chocolates, I mentally simulate Sally's mental processes, her having certain perceptions and thereby acquiring certain beliefs. In other words, I imagine being in Sally's situation, responding as she responds. When I engage with fiction I simulate the process of acquiring beliefs—the beliefs I would acquire if I took the work I am engaged with for fact rather than fiction. Here I imagine myself acquiring factual knowledge. In the Sally case I imagine being in the situation someone else actually is in; in the fiction case I imagine being a situation I could be in but actually am not in. In the first case the imagining is an instrument to a further purpose: to inform me of the mental processes of someone else. In the second case the imagining has no further purpose: the simulation provoked by the fiction is simply something I enjoy. (Currie 1995: 148)

There are two claims here on which Currie could rest his distinction between fiction and non-fiction. The first is: 'When I engage with fiction I simulate the process of acquiring beliefs—the beliefs I would acquire if I took the work I am engaged with for fact rather than fiction'. In other words, the scenario I simulate is that of acquiring beliefs by reading the book in front of me—simulating the process of reading the book as non-fiction.

It might be that 'reading the book as non-fiction' involves simulating its content (perhaps the book is a first-hand account of being attacked by a lion). In this case, I would simulate being in the position of someone simulating the events in the book. As Currie himself has argued, simulation exhibits 'the collapse of iterativity': imagining being someone imagining that p collapses into imagining that p (Currie 1995: 158–9). Hence, Currie's account of reading fiction would simply be simulating being a situation. What was going on in the head of the reader of fiction would be no different from what was going on in the head of the reader of non-fiction.

We cannot leave the matter there, as it might it be that non-fictions that provoke simulations are in some way uncharacteristic. Let us look at a different case, and take as our example of non-fiction the last moments of Conolly and Stoddart in Bukhara (as related by Peter Hopkirk).

First, while a silent crowd looked on, the two British officers were made to dig their own graves. Then they were ordered to kneel down and to prepare for death. Colonel Stoddart, after loudly denouncing the tyranny of the Emir, was the first to be beheaded. Next the executioner turned to Conolly and informed him that the Emir had offered to spare his life if he would renounce Christianity and embrace Islam. Aware that Stoddart's forcible conversion had not saved him from imprisonment and death, Conolly, a devout Christian, replied: 'Colonel Stoddart has been a Mussulman for three years and you have killed him. I will not become one, and I am ready to die.' He then stretched out his neck for the executioner, and a moment later his head rolled in the dust beside that of his friend. (Hopkirk 1990: 278)

What goes on in the reader's head when they engage with this as non-fiction? Let us assume that these propositions end up as beliefs, but what if anything happens before that? One possibility is that nothing does: we simply read the text and acquire beliefs. However, non-fiction is surely no different from fiction in our dwelling on its content and that content engaging our affective reactions. As much as any fiction these propositions 'work their own affects on our mental economy'. If we examine what goes on when we read Hopkirk's description it looks very much like Currie's description of simulation. Our mental states are not caused by perceiving Conolly and Stoddard and there is certainly no action with respect to those men. It is true that the scenario is an actual, but, as we have seen, there is no bar to simulating actual scenarios. It is difficult to see where Currie could locate any difference between what a reader does with a fiction and what a reader does with a non-fiction. If this is right, it is difficult to make sense of the claim that reading the former is a matter of simulating reading the latter.

Matters are not clarified by Currie's more detailed description of our engagement with fiction. Currie distinguishes two kinds of imaginings: primary imaginings and secondary imaginings. Primary imaginings are 'imagining those things that make it fictional, as *Anna Karenina* makes it fictional that Anna commits suicide' (Currie 1995: 152). It is difficult to know what Currie means by 'primary imagining' as the only account we have been given is of imagining in terms of simulation and, as we have seen, simulation has no particular connection with fiction. However, it is secondary imagination that interests me here: '*Secondary* imagining occurs when we imagine various things so as to imagine what is true in the story' (Currie 1995: 152). Currie goes on to provide an example:

It is when we are able, in imagination, to feel as the character feels that fictions of character take hold of us. This process of empathetic re-enactment of the character's situation is what I call secondary imagining. As a result of putting myself, in imagination, in the character's position, I come to have imaginary versions of the thoughts, feelings and attitudes I would have were I in that situation. Having identified those thoughts, feelings and attitudes ostensively, I am then able to imagine that the character felt *that* way. That is how secondary imagining is a guide to primary imagining.(Currie 1995: 153–4)

There is no reason to deny that this occurs (although, as we will see, there are reasons not to use the term 'imagination' to describe it). However, for familiar reasons, this will have nothing in particular to do with fiction. Let us use Currie's own example of 'a certain character walking down a dark street' (Currie 1995: 153). All sides agree that the same sequence of words can appear in a fiction or a non-fiction, so if I need to use the secondary imagination to guide myself through that sequence of words ('If the dark street hides something threatening, the character who walks it may have thoughts, anxieties, visual and auditory experiences and bodily sensations that it would be important for readers to imagine something about') I will need to use it whether it appears in a fiction or a non-fiction. It is difficult to see what could justify the claim that secondary imagination is used in reading Raymond Chandler but not used in reading the account of the death of Stoddart and Conolly.

The second claim on which Currie could rest his distinction between fiction and non-fiction is present in the sentence 'In the Sally case I imagine being in the situation someone else actually is in; in the fiction case I imagine being a situation I could be in but actually am not in'. Currie here accepts that the simulated scenario can be either actual or not actual, and links non-fictional cases with the former and fictional cases with the latter. This would effectively give up the consensus view, as it links non-fiction and fiction equally to the imagination. In effect, it bypasses the imagination and defines fictions as narratives that deal with situations believed to be non-actual. However, such a definition is patently inadequate, as Currie himself has argued (Currie 1990: 4–9).

There is one further section of Currie's account which is difficult to interpret.

> I said that what makes something a belief rather than some other kind of state is its causes and effects. In that case there is something unsatisfactory in my description of simulation as 'running beliefs off-line'... Running off-line is, exactly, a matter of severing the connections between our mental states and their perceptual causes and behavioural effects. A belief run 'off-line' isn't really a belief, just as a monarch who has been deposed is no longer a monarch. Revolutions transmute monarchs into ex-monarchs. Simulation transmutes beliefs into imaginings. Just as a belief and a desire may have the same content but differ functionally, so may a belief and an imagining. Believing that it will rain has certain connections to perception and behaviour which, when they are severed, transmutes the belief into a case of imagining that it will rain. (Currie 1995: 149)[2]

It is difficult to see how this is consistent with the fact that simulated scenarios can be actual and hence believed to be true. The only way to make them consistent is to take Currie to be spelling things out in terms of token

---

[2] This view is also suggested by the discussion in Currie 1995: 160.

rather than type mental states. I believe that General Allenby dismounted and walked when he entered Jerusalem in 1917 (let us call this p). However, when I am reading a representation of this the token of p that is in my mind does not have a standard perceptual input and is not hooked up to any motivations to action: it is being run off-line. Hence, I have the type belief p, but the token currently operative in my mental economy is not a belief but a make-belief. However, this view appears to contradict other claims that Currie makes in which he contrasts newspapers and documentaries (which involve beliefs) and fictions (which involve the imagination) (Currie 1995: 148). On this interpretation, each would equally involve the imagination. Furthermore, it is repudiated in the later work (with Ian Ravenscroft) where the idea that 'imaginings were beliefs-that-also-occupy-imagination-defining-roles' is explicitly rejected (Currie and Ravenscroft 2002: 18). Most tellingly, however, it would also mean giving up the consensus view as the imagination would no more be linked to fiction than it would be linked to non-fiction.

The conclusion I draw from this is that Currie has argued for one view (that all mental states taken off-line are imaginings and not beliefs) and mistaken it for a second view (that all and only mental states that arise from reading fictional propositions are imaginings and not beliefs). It is the second view that entails that there is a link between fiction and imagination. However, no argument is provided for the second view and, furthermore, it is incompatible with the first view for which arguments are provided.

Although Currie has not changed his position significantly in the later book (written with Ian Ravenscroft) there is more detail. He is still concerned, as am I, with 'the recreative imagination' which is distinct from 'the creative imagination', the latter being 'the capacity to do things in a new way' (Currie and Ravenscroft 2002: 10). He links the recreative imagination (hereafter simply 'the imagination') with 'perspective-shifting' (Currie and Ravenscroft 2002: 9), and comes up with an explicit definition:

Imaginative projection involves the capacity to have, and in good measure to control the having of, states that are not perceptions or beliefs or decisions or experiences of movements of one's body, but which are in various ways like those states—like them in ways that enable the states possessed through imagination to mimic and, relative to certain purposes, to substitute for perceptions, beliefs, decisions, and experiences of movements. (Currie and Ravenscroft 2002: 11)

This is an unhealthy amalgam of the two views separated above. There is the view associated with perspective-shifting: imagining involves visualizing as opposed to perceiving and an absence of connection to action ('experiences of movements'). There is also the second view, which has not been argued for, that links imagination with fiction: imaginings are contrasted with beliefs. This confusion underpins the rest of their discussion. Immediately after giving the definition Currie and Ravenscroft contrast 'visual imagery' with 'visual experience', 'auditory imaging' with 'hearing things', 'tactile imagery' with 'touching things', and 'motor imagery' with 'the experience of moving one's body'. This clearly refers to the first, perspective-shifting, view and is nothing to do with the division between fiction and non-fiction: clearly there is no connection between our having visual, auditory, tactile, or motor imagery and that imagery being fictional.

The confusion becomes even more stark when Currie and Ravenscroft consider a problem from Hume's discussion of tragedy. The problem is that our engagement with tragedies typically manifests a prima facie contradiction. We desire that the heroine be saved but (as we are averse to happy endings) we do not desire that the narrative end with the heroine being saved. Let us call this 'the dissonance problem'. Currie and Ravenscroft solve this problem by distinguishing between an internal and an external perspective on the play: we have a 'desire-like imagining' that the heroine be saved yet we desire that the narrative does not end happily. I will need to say something in response to this problem in due course (indeed, in Chapter 5). However, that is not the issue that concerns me here. Rather, it is the fact that—as my view would predict—the dissonance problem occurs with both non-fictional and fictional narratives. It arises for Cicero's story of the butchery of the Sicilian captains which, as Hume points out, is non-fiction and taken to be so: the audience are 'convinced of the reality of every circumstance' (Currie and Ravenscroft 2002: 203).[3] Currie and Ravenscroft solve the dissonance problem within their account of how we engage with fictional narratives. How do they solve it with respect to non-fictional narratives?

Currie and Ravenscroft wisely reject the option of 'treating the stories as if they were fiction'. If we standardly treated non-fictional narratives as fiction, the distinction between non-fictional and fictional narratives would

---

[3] The original can be found in Hume 1993: 128.

be lost. Instead, they argue that 'the narrator's art is such as to generate in me narrative desires such as the desire that this story turn out badly for the characters concerned... the response is to the narrative of the events, and not to the events themselves' (Currie and Ravenscroft 2002: 204). However, it is not clear that the second option is substantially different from the first. Their position appears to be that the relevant mental states (be they desire-like imaginings or belief-like imaginings) are generated by the narrative whether the narrative is non-fiction or fiction. In this discussion at least, it appears the first view (that imagination involves perspective shifting independent of the divide between non-fiction and fiction) has been preferred to the second view (that the imagination arises from our engagement with fiction rather than non-fiction).

So far, in my investigation of Currie's work, I have found nothing to support the claim that the imagination contrasts with belief and hence has a particular link to fiction. There are two further arguments to consider. Although the first of these rests on a mistake, the second does raise an issue for which I do not so far have an explanation.

The first argument appears in the context of a discussion concerning the 'capacity of imaginings to mirror the inferential patterns of belief' (Currie and Ravenscroft 2002: 13). This is an interesting issue to which I will return presently. In setting up the argument, Currie and Ravenscroft make the familiar point that readers need to 'fill out' narratives with background information.

If you imagine the novel's hero in London one day and in Chicago the next, you will also imagine that she flew there, unless there is some strong indication that she got there by another means. (Currie and Ravenscroft 2002: 13)

Currie and Ravenscroft assume that what is explicit in the narrative is what we imagine and that we fill out the narrative from our beliefs: 'we... draw on our beliefs to fill out what the story tells us'. Once they make a number of plausible assumptions, this enables Currie and Ravenscroft to conclude that 'imaginings [are] inferentially commensurate with beliefs'. As my view does not contrast imaginings with beliefs in our engaging with representations, I do not have this problem (I shall discuss this in the next chapter). My purpose here is only to indicate Currie and Ravenscroft's contrast between what is explicit (imaginings) and what is appealed to in order to fill out the gaps (beliefs). If this were correct, it would provide a contrast between imaginings and beliefs. However, it is not correct. Any narrative, whether fiction or non-fiction, has a contrast between what is explicit and what needs to be 'filled out'. With non-fictional narratives and some fictional narratives (broadly, those that are 'realistic') we appeal to our background beliefs. With some fictional narratives (broadly those that are 'non-realistic') the background could be filled out by beliefs or by things that are 'true in the story' but which we do not believe. The contrast between what is explicit and what needs to be filled out in a narrative is not the contrast between imagination and belief, nor does it mark anything true of fictional narratives that is not also true of non-fictional narratives. I shall consider this further in Chapter 6.

The second argument concerns the different roles imaginings and beliefs have in our mental economy. Currie and Ravenscroft mention two. First, they contrast the different relations imaginings and beliefs have with respect to motivation: 'imagination does not have the motivational force of belief; we do not act on our imaginings as we act on our beliefs' (Currie and Ravenscroft 2002: 16). I shall say more about this below but, as we have seen, non-fictional simulated scenarios are no more or less related to action than fictional simulated scenarios. Thus, in the relevant cases, the relation of imagination to motivation is that same as that of belief. The second concerns contradictory beliefs: 'belief…is normative in that an agent who has contradictory beliefs (in any sense of 'belief') is in a less than ideal epistemic situation. It is no defect in an agent's epistemic condition that she imagines thing contrary to what she believes' (Currie and Ravenscroft 2002: 17). I will only be able to give a full answer to this after I have presented my positive account of engaging with narratives in Chapters 5 and 6. However, I hope I can say enough now to blunt the force of this argument. Recall that the contrast Currie and Ravenscroft are arguing for, and which I deny, is that *in our engagement with narratives* the non-fictional case is different from the fictional case in that the former involve beliefs and the latter involving imaginings—which are held to be a different type of mental state. Their argument here is that beliefs are constrained by a requirement of consistency and imaginings are not constrained by a requirement of consistency.

Currie and Ravenscroft's point brings to the fore the fundamental flaw in the consensus view. The view takes itself to be distinguishing between two sorts of representation: non-fictional and fictional. More often than not it is addressing a different distinction: between our engaging the world and our engaging representations. I do not dispute that an agent who has contradictory beliefs is in a less than ideal epistemic situation. However, that is not the point at issue. The point at issue is whether the epistemic constraints that govern engaging with non-fictional narratives are different to the epistemic constraints that govern engaging fictional narratives. The epistemic constraint that governs our engaging with narratives is that we need to have some pro-attitude[4] to the propositions that form the content of the narrative. Currie and Ravenscroft's constraint is simply a special case of this; a special case that applies to non-fictional narratives and realistic fictional narratives. Even in the case of non-realistic fictional narratives there will be *some* epistemic constraint; no narrative will simply allow us to form what pro-attitudes we like. To be clear: the point at issue is what would count as being in a less than ideal epistemic situation *with respect to the content of a narrative*. This, I contend, is the same for non-fictional and fictional narratives: have a pro-attitude to those propositions that form the content of the narrative. Of course, a further question arises as to the relation between our pro-attitudes towards the content of the narrative and our pre-existing structures of belief. However, this issue (which I will discuss in Chapter 7) should not be confused with the quite separate issue being discussed here.

The second account of the imagination I shall consider is that of Aaron Meskin and Jonathan Weinberg. Meskin and Weinberg are engaged in an investigation of the difference between what they claim are our 'affective responses to fiction' and 'its non-fictive analogue'; of presenting 'a theory of the cognitive imagination as it functions in our engagement with fiction' (Meskin and Weinberg 2006: 222). In search of the structure of the cognitive imagination, they consider the affective responses that fictions elicit, which they call 'fictive affect'. 'Fictive affect' has certain characteristics which Meskin and Weinberg hope will provide a functional characterization of the mental state that marks it as different to that of belief. According to Meskin and Weinberg, those subject to fictive affect 'will fail to demonstrate... [certain] behaviours that would be expected of someone experiencing its nonfictive analogue'.

... we do not (generally) find audience members behaving fully as they do when they have emotional responses in ordinary (i.e., nonfictive) life. Horror movie

---

[4] I shall use this neutral term here, which I will elucidate below. It is not too misleading to think of this as 'imagine', provided you bear in mind that imagining the content of narratives is neutral between non-fiction and fiction.

viewers do not typically flee the cinema screaming. (Meskin and Weinberg 2006: 224)

Such considerations drive them to two substantial conclusions. The first is what they call '*minimal nondoxastic cognitivism* (MNC)':

(1) the mental representations of the cognitive imagination share the basic syntactic and semantic properties of beliefs, and (2) they can interact with both the inferential and affective systems in much the same way as beliefs, but (3) they lack other of the causal properties of beliefs, especially the capacity to direct our action-control systems. (Meskin and Weinberg 2006: 225)

The second is that there is 'a distinct representational system in which the imagined contents are entertained' (Meskin and Weinberg 2006: 231):

This 'imagination system' is very similar to the belief system, but with key differences rendering it appropriate for MNC. The representations in the imagination system are of just the same form as beliefs; for example, they are propositional. Furthermore (and in virtue of this), imagined contents interact causally with many of the same systems, and in much the same way, that beliefs do. For example, both systems can take input from the perceptual systems, and both systems can input to and receive output from our inferential systems. Moreover, both systems can drive our affect systems. But the two systems are not functionally identical. Importantly, the imagination system is not connected to the action guidance system in the way that the belief system is. And, of course, the general function of the imagination is not to represent the world as it is (as is the function of belief) (Meskin and Weinberg 2006: 231)

This heavy philosophical machinery can be summed up as four claims: the imagination is processed in a different system from belief; the imagination and belief share basic syntactic and semantic features; the imagination and belief differ systematically in relation to action; and that it is the function of beliefs and not imaginative states to 'represent the world as it is'.

The need for an 'imagination system' disappears once one accepts that non-fictional and fictional simulated scenarios have identical relations to action.[5] The second need not concern us here, as we have yet to establish a difference between imagination and belief. It is the third and fourth of these that distinguish beliefs and imaginings. It is clear that, with respect to the third, Meskin and Weinberg are subject to the same confusion as

---

[5] Faced with this problem Currie and Ravenscroft postulate a single mechanism but with different entrances and exits (Currie and Ravenscroft 2002: 68). Obviously, this too is unnecessary.

Currie. Certainly the members of the audience of a film do not 'flee the cinema screaming', but that is because (in Currie's terms) they are running their mental states 'off line'. The relevant point is that the inputs are 'disconnected from their normal sensory inputs and behavioural outputs'. This is true whether or not the inputs are fiction or non-fiction. Put another way, it is true that horror movie viewers do not typically flee the cinema screaming, but neither do documentary viewers, television news viewers, or any other kind of viewer. Like Currie, Meskin and Weinberg are characterizing a type of mental state (a DCA or an imagining) in ways that are neutral as to whether the source of that state is a fictional representation or a non-fictional representation and then used it to define fiction.

Unlike the first three, Meskin and Weinberg's fourth claim does not fall at the first hurdle. However, it will need some careful reconstruction. In as much as the imagination is linked to simulation, its general purpose is exactly to 'represent the world as it is'; we run our beliefs 'off line' in order to discover how the world goes. However, it is certainly true that the class of propositions we can simulate is greater than the class of propositions we believe. We do not take the propositions we simulate but do not believe to 'represent the world as it is'. However, as before, this cannot be used as the basis for a definition of fiction as we would already need to know the proposition we were simulating was fictional in order not to believe it. Furthermore, as I shall discuss presently, this has no very clear relation to fiction. There are plenty of propositions in non-fiction we do not believe (including metaphors, hyperbole, and other literary tropes) and plenty of propositions in fiction we straightforwardly believe. Nonetheless, there is clearly an issue here. Some of the propositions we imagine start off as beliefs, or end up as beliefs, or both, and some of the propositions we imagine do not. As I have conceded, any account of our engaging with representations, whether non-fictional or fictional, needs to take this into account. I shall provide my account of this in Chapter 7.

That fictions contain propositions we straightforwardly believe is a prima facie problem for the consensus view. So far in this chapter, my argument has been negative: that, on their own account of the imagination the consensus view has no reason to link the imagination with fiction. For the remainder of this chapter I shall go on the offensive and examine the difficulties for the consensus view of a self-inflicted problem: if the imagination is defined in contrast to belief, how is it that they work seamlessly together? The content of any fictional representation will be a mixture of propositions that are true in the fiction and also true *simpliciter* and propositions that are true in the fiction and not true *simpliciter*. The former are not, in Walton's words, 'interruptions in the fiction, interpolations of nonfiction woven into an otherwise fictional fabric' (Walton 1990: 79). In terms of what is going on when we read, we cannot treat the two in a way that would entail a difference in the reader's experience.

To see what this would say about fictional works that include propositions we take to be true *simpliciter*, consider the standard example: *War and Peace*. Part II of that book opens with the following proposition:

p: In October 1805, Russian troops were occupying the towns and villages of the Archduchy of Austria.

Further on in the chapter we have the following:

q: The regimental commander was an elderly, sanguine general with grizzled eyebrows and side-whiskers.

p is true is true-in-*War and Peace*, true *simpliciter*, and (let us assume) known to be true by the reader. q is true-in-*War and Peace* and not true *simpliciter*. It seems the consensus view has three options in describing what is going on as we read the opening of Part II: we imagine that p and believe that p; we imagine that p and do not believe that p; we do not imagine that p but do believe that p. I shall consider each in turn.

It is not a problem for the first of the three options that it entails that we can have different propositional attitudes towards the same content. Consider the content that 'I have a Ducati motorbike'. I can believe this, desire this, hope this, or even—in some bizarre set of circumstances—fear this. It is even not a problem that the view requires something stronger: that we can *simultaneously* have different propositional attitudes (believing and imagining) to the same content. There are some propositional attitudes (for example, believing that p and desiring that p) which—pathological cases aside—we cannot hold simultaneously. There are others (for example, believing that p and regretting that p) we can hold simultaneously. The case is delicate with believing and imagining as the consensus view frequently (although as we have seen, not invariably) defines them in contrast to each other.

If the problem is not that we have two different attitudes to the same content then what is the problem? It is that the view mis-characterizes the situation. To see this, let us examine a well known experiment by Alan

Leslie to which the consensus view appeals for support. Here is Shaun Nichols' view as to the compatibility between belief and imagination (which Nichols calls 'pretense').

> Several features of the theory can be illustrated with a lovely experiment on children by Alan Leslie. In Leslie's experiment, the child pretends to fill two cups with tea. The experimenter picks up one of the cups, upends it, and places it next to the other cup. Then the experimenter asks the child to point at the 'full cup' and at the 'empty cup'. Both cups are really empty throughout the entire procedure, but two-year-olds reliably indicate that the 'empty cup' is the one that had been turned upside down and the 'full cup' is the other one. One significant feature of episodes like Leslie's tea party is that children distinguish what is pretend from what is real. That is, at no point in this experiment do children believe that either of the cups is full. Their pretense that the cup is full is 'quarantined' from their belief that the cup is not full. Another, more interesting, feature of the experiment is that it indicates that a belief and a pretense can have exactly the same *content*. When the children are asked to point to the 'empty cup' and the 'full cup,' they maintain that the previously overturned cup is the empty one. On the most natural interpretation of this, the child is *pretending that the cup is empty*. We adopt the representationalist approach that is common in this area and say that such pretending involves a 'pretense representation' with the content *the cup is empty*. Although the child is pretending that the cup is empty, she is not blind to the fact that the cup is really empty throughout; rather, the child also *believes that the cup is empty*. This suggests that the crucial difference between pretense representations and beliefs is not given by the *content* of the representation. For a pretense representation and a belief can have exactly the same content. So, pretense representations are quarantined from beliefs, and yet the distinction is not driven by differences in content. The natural cognitivist proposal, then, is that pretense representations differ from belief representations by their *function*. Just as desires are distinguished from beliefs by their characteristic functional roles, so too pretenses are distinguished from beliefs. (Nichols 2004: 129–30).[6]

In the case Leslie describes the content is 'that the cup is empty,' and the child both believes it is empty (in the actual world) and imagines it is empty (in the tea-party game). The child believes the tea-cup is empty of tea but imagines it is empty of make-believe tea. The two are, as Nichols says, distinguished by their functional roles. Furthermore, they are 'quarantined': the child would be mistaken to transfer the state of affairs from its 'pretend box' to its 'belief box'. This is not analogous to the case we are considering. Here the content is that in October 1805, Russian troops were occupying the towns and villages of the Archduchy of Austria. This

---

[6] The original experiment is in Leslie (1994).

is, before we read the passage in the novel, a dispositional belief. As we read the passage in the novel its functional role does not change (except in as much as it changes from a dispositional belief to an occurrent belief). Furthermore, its role qua dispositional belief is not 'quarantined' from its role qua proposition in *War and Peace*. It occupies our attention while we read the novel, but is (to use the boxology jargon) a perfectly respectable citizen of our belief box. *Something* needs to be said about the relation between the non-occurrent tokens of our beliefs and the occurrent tokens of our beliefs (when they form part of the content of a narrative with which we are engaged) but this cannot be modelled on the situation described in Leslie's experiment. I return to this in Chapter 7.

The consensus view of the compatibility of believing and imagining has recently been given a sophisticated restatement by Kathleen Stock.[7] Stock believes that, necessarily, a fictive utterance prescribes imagining (Stock 2011: 146). In essence, Stock distinguishes (for some proposition p) believing that p from imagining that p in terms of some set of propositions of which p is a part. Clearly, the same proposition can be a part of different sets hence the same proposition can be the content of both a belief and an imagining. She attempts to establish this with two claims concerning imagining.

CONNECT 1: Necessarily, a thinker T who imagines that p is disposed to connect her thought that p is the case with other propositional thoughts about what is the case. (Stock 2011: 151)

And

CONNECT 2: Necessarily, where a thinker T imagines that p at time t, either T does not believe that p *or* T is disposed to connect her thought that p is the case to some further proposition(s) about what is the case, whose content is not replicated by any belief of hers at t. (Stock 2011: 153)

Stock is clear that she 'does not purport to offer a complete functional analysis of imagining' (Stock 2011: 153). With that caveat in mind, I am going to push her view a little further—not in a way she would herself— to see if we can learn anything about the imagination. I shall omit references to time for the sake of simplicity. CONNECT 2 suggests that

---

[7] Stock herself thinks reference to the Leslie experiment is inadequate to defend the consensus view (Stock 2011: 150-1).

a functional account of propositional imagining (which is the type of imagining with which Stock is concerned) is a disjunction. The first disjunct is that X imagines that p if (1) X entertains that p and (2) X does not believe that p. This is unhelpful as an account of imagining, as all it tells us is that imagination is not identical to belief. The second has more substance: X imagines that p if (1) X entertains that p (2) X is disposed to connect her thought that p with further propositions about what is the case and (3) amongst those further propositions will be at least one she does not believe. Belief and imagination would share (1) and (2); the suggested difference between them lies in (3). To make the contrast, for the case of belief, (3) would need to be (3*): all those further propositions will be ones that we believe. Let us return to CONNECT 1. The plausibility of this depends on how strongly we read 'disposed'. As Stock herself argues, the only credible reading is a weak reading: the disposition itself may be unactualized (Stock 2011: 154). This puts a great deal of pressure on the difference between (3) and (3*). Let us grant that the thought that p disposes us to further thoughts connected with p. However, the question of whether, amongst those propositions that one has an unactualized disposition to think, there is or is not one that fails to be a belief, is surely unanswerable. It is certainly an unlikely basis for any interesting distinction.

Perhaps Stock's view could be strengthened specifying the relevant sets of propositions in a different way.

X imagines that p if (1) X entertains that p (2) X is disposed to connect her thought that p with further propositions about what is the case and (3) those further propositions are given by R, where R is the content of the representation that is the source of X's entertaining that p, and (4) R is fictional if the content of R contains at least one proposition that X does not believe.

Stock wisely rejects this approach as it is clear that the definition in (4) is inadequate (Stock 2011: 159). As Stacie Friend has pointed out, most non-fictional representations will contain at least one proposition a reader does not believe (Friend 2011: 171).

Let us then consider the second view: that we imagine that p and do not believe that p. This is the view Currie puts forward in *Image and Mind* (quoted earlier): 'A belief run 'off-line' isn't really a belief, just as a monarch who has been deposed is no longer a monarch. Revolutions transmute monarchs into ex-monarchs. Simulation transmutes beliefs into imaginings' (Currie 1995: 148). I argued earlier that not only could this view not be defended, it has also been explicitly repudiated by Currie. This leaves the third view: that we do not imagine that p but we do believe that p. Perhaps for reason just canvassed, Currie appears to have shifted to this view in his later work:

> As readers, we let our imaginings mingle with our beliefs, and further imaginings emerge that, so far as their contents go, are identical with what would emerge from the operation of inference on belief alone. (Currie and Ravenscroft 2002: 13)

Reading *War and Peace* involves bringing to mind two different sorts of mental state: those such as p which are beliefs and those such as q which are imaginings. To avoid running foul of Walton's 'interruption' stricture, there must be no difference in the reader's experience between believing that p and imagining that q. This does not imply that propositions that are that are believed are *processed* in the same way as propositions that are imagined, as differences in processing may not show up in the reader's experience. It does, however, raise the question of what the difference between the attitudes to p and q amounts to. There is no difference in the type of input (we read both p and q), there is no difference in the relation to motivation (we act on neither p nor q), and there is no difference in the reader's experience. What, then, does this option amount to? Presumably, when reading a text, a reader is building a mental model of its content. With respect to engaging with the narrative, the propositions take their place in this mental model whether they are beliefs or imaginings (that is, they work seamlessly together). What marks some as beliefs and some as imaginings? The distinction is only that, when we engage with representations (non-fictional or fictional) some propositions bear a different relation to our pre-existing structures of belief than do others. Roughly, some are either already in such structures or are heading towards such structures and others are not. This seems clearly right and I have already conceded it needs to be part of any account. This does not give us a distinction between two types of mental state, however. The claim is only that, of those propositions in the mental model, some of them we will also believe.

For completeness, I should mention again the problem that arises from taking this option. If we concede that what we pre-theoretically think of as fictional works contain a patchwork of propositions we are mandated to believe as well as propositions we are mandated to imagine, it looks as if we cannot define fictional *work* as a work that contains propositions we are mandated to imagine. The solution to this problem—the classification problem—is much debated by those who hold the consensus view. It is a difficult problem, and I will put their findings to my own use in Chapter 7.

4

The Real Distinction

In this chapter I hope to provide a convincing case for restructuring the philosophy of fiction; to shift the focus from the divide between non-fiction and fiction to the focus on the divide between situations in which action (of a sort) is possible and situations in which action is not possible. I shall begin with a slippery-slope argument. This, like all slippery-slope arguments, does not establish its conclusion but I hope it will make a prima-facie case for the position. Let us take as our example stories about wolves and caves.[1] Consider a simple case of testimony: somebody runs into my cave and tells me that there are a dozen wolves, about a mile away, which are heading in my direction. There are various questions that arise about testimony, such as the grounds of the warrant of the transmitted belief, but they need not detain us here. The issue is the nature of the psychological resources required for my understanding what I am being told. I take it that nobody would think that the imagination need be among those resources: I simply hear the sentence, and, understanding English, acquire a new belief.

Now consider another situation. Instead of somebody coming to tell me that a wolf is on its way, I tell the assembled family about what happened when a wolf came into my grandfather's cave, many years ago. Let us assume that the story is accurate. There are many ways in which I could tell the story. At one extreme, I could simply be using it as a template of what to do (or what not to do) if a wolf came into the cave. 'Grandfather engaged the wolf at the mouth of the cave, which meant that Johnny could not run out to get help. So if a wolf comes into the cave in future, we should let it come all the way in before trying to hit it with the axe, so somebody can slip out behind it.' At the other extreme, I could be telling the story to

---

[1] None of what follows is an attempt on natural history nor an attempt to provide support for my argument by speculation as to what happened to our ancestors in the Pleistocene.

entertain the family as the long winter evening stretches out: 'Once, when Grandfather was a lad, he was just settling down for the evening when he heard a noise…' and so on. Without suggesting that the distinction is one of kind, rather than degree, let us call the first a 'thin' experience of a representation and the second a 'thick' experience of a representation.[2] I shall sometimes call representations that characteristically provide thick experiences 'thick representations' and those that characteristically provide thin experiences 'thin representations'.

The slippery slope is that it does not seem a big jump from representing events that either are happening or have happened to counterfactual representations. Consider a situation in which we are interviewing for head of the village. 'Suppose a wolf came into your cave,' asks one questioner, 'what would you do?' The potential mayor could appeal to history, and relate what he or she did last time. Alternatively, he or she could relate what Smith did in his successful defence of his cave against a wolf, and avow to follow that precedent. However, the potential mayor could also answer the question directly: 'Were a wolf to come into my cave, I would send the small children to the back of the cave while at the same time crossing to get my axe' and so on. Instead of content of the representation being what did happen, the content is what could happen. It is difficult to see why the psychology of understanding the former is going to be very different from the psychology of understanding the latter.

In my example, the potential mayor has provided a thin representation: he or she has made a supposition ('were a wolf to come into my cave…') and is reasoning within the scope of that supposition. However, we could easily imagine how such a representation could become thick. Consider a case in which the village meeting is deciding on what to spend their meagre resources: decorations to the village cave or defences against wolves. One of the villagers, in favour of the latter proposal, gets up and spins a terrifying tale of the consequences of a pack of wolves getting to the heart of the village: men and women savaged, children chewed to pieces, the streets running with blood. Chastened, the villagers vote for the wolf defences and art has to wait another few decades to get a start in history.

---

[2] I apologize to John Gibson for using these terms to mark a different distinction to the one for which he uses them (Gibson 2011). I have tried to think of others, but none have seemed appropriate.

It is another small move from this kind of representation to fiction. Having bored the family with the history of the time the wolf got into Grandfather's cave, it strikes me that, as the point is to pass the long winter evenings, I need not be constrained by truth. 'Once upon a time, in a village far away, but in a cave a little like this one, two ferocious wolves came running in…' and so on. As suggested, my goal could be entertainment. However, it could also be edification: as a matter of fact, no wolf has ever run into the cave but (like the querulous villager) if I spin a tale about a wolf wreaking havoc I might succeed in making my family less complacent about keeping track of the axe. In either case, whether entertainment or edification, there is a point to my making the representation thick.

My view, in short, is that representations can be put to different uses: to teach, to persuade and to entertain being three of them. Representations also come in two varieties, thin and thick; or, rather, representations exist along a continuum from the very thin to the very thick. The traditional distinction, between representations that are fiction and representations that are non-fiction, is entirely unhelpful. It does not match any intuitive divide amongst the above. Regardless of what we have said so far, it is independently implausible to think that what goes on when we read fiction is very different from what goes on when we read non-fiction. To hold that, one would need to hold that there are issues that arise in our engaging with *War and Peace* which do not arise with our engaging with (for example) *With Napoleon in Russia* by Faber de Faur (described by the publisher as 'vivid and gripping memoirs of the campaign'). We can certainly grant that the relation between the former and subsequent belief is less straightforward than the relation between the latter and subsequent belief but apart from that they have more or less everything else in common.

Although my discussion in the earlier chapters was mainly negative— showing the failure of attempts to demonstrate an interesting connection between fiction and the imagination—of more significance is the positive point: that there is an important distinction here but it is not between non-fiction and fiction, but between (to introduce some terminology) 'confrontations' and 'representations'. Roughly, confrontations are situations in which action is possible. Representations are situations in which action is not possible because what is being represented to us is out of reach.[3]

---

[3] The view that this is the fundamental distinction here is also held by Richard Gerrig: 'What appears to matter, therefore, is not so much whether the danger is fictional or nonfictional but whether overt action is functional in the circumstances' (Gerrig 1993: 189).

First, I shall attempt to be more precise about confrontations (or, as I will sometimes say, about 'being in a confrontation relation'). Human beings come in a rather nice little package for negotiating their immediate environments. Using our five regular senses (particularly sight and sound) we form beliefs about what is going on around us. If a wolf comes into the cave, we usually see that a wolf has come into the cave. Seeing that a wolf has come into the cave gives us several beliefs: not only about its size, shape, and colour, but its spatial location relative to ourselves. These beliefs, together with various other mental states such as a desire not to be bitten by a wolf, cause action. We are possessed of limbs that enable us to run out of the cave or run across the cave to grab the axe. We are possessed of onboard means of communicating: we can shout at the wolf in an attempt to frighten it off, or we can shout so as to summon help or warn our family not to come into the cave.

In order to be in a confrontation relation with an object we have to know that the object is there and be aware of its location relative to ourselves. In the usual circumstances we can use this knowledge to act towards the object. We might not be able to act because we might lack the right 'instrumental beliefs'; that is, those beliefs that would enable us to transform our desire to act into action (Matravers 1998: 22). For example, if I am paralysed or tied to the stake I might have no instrumental beliefs that will enable my desire not to be harmed to be turned into avoiding or combating the wolf. All in all, with our senses, our mental states, our motivations, our means of communication, and our limbs, we are well equipped to deal with things that happen around us. This is not a cosmic coincidence of course; if we were not well equipped to deal with happenings in our immediate environment we would have died out.[4]

Here are two more characteristics of confrontations. First, we do not usually need special explanations for acting during confrontations. That is, if confronted with something of the type that calls for action (a wolf running into the cave) we do not need some additional explanation of why we react. Of course, there might be cases in which an explanation is needed for an action: 'the reason he smote the dog was that he thought it was a wolf'. In addition, an explanation could be provided; it is only that it would be rather a tedious bit of belief/desire psychology: 'the reason he smote the wolf was that he believed he was endangered by the wolf and

---

[4] I am grateful to Neil Sinhababu for pressing me on these issues.

desired not to be so endangered'. Finally, there is an interesting discussion to be had concerning the line between states of affairs that call for action and states of affairs that do not. The closer that line is approached the more an explanation is needed. It will be easier to explain being late for dinner because one gave a colleague a lift home if that colleague was your elderly friend with the dodgy hip, than if that colleague was the self-reliant yet unfeasibly gorgeous new graduate student. Second, as is familiar from moral philosophy, the fact that something happens in our immediate environment may put us under an obligation to act. That is, even if, as the above paragraph claims, we need no special explanation as to why we act it could be true of us that we ought to act. I am not obliged to go around looking for children who have fallen into ponds, but if a child falls into a pond in my immediate environment then, all things being equal, I am obliged to rescue him or her.

This neat little package of noticing things and then dealing with them with our onboard resources can come apart. My eyes give me information about things happening at distances from me which make direct action impossible. For example, I might see a child falling into a pond but he or she is in the valley and I am on the hill. We can use artificial devices to extend our epistemological reach. With a telescope, I can see the wolf coming from several miles away which gives me time to warn other people or form a reception committee. I can place microphones in the trees and hear whether intruders are lurking in the woods, or cameras in the trees and see whether intruders are lurking in the woods. According to Kendall Walton, I can see things vast distances away in time and space by means of photographs. That is, a camera captures the appearance of an object and records it on paper. Transferring the paper to our immediate environment, we are able to see the object (Walton 1984). Furthermore, I can extend my capacity to act. I can get a long stick to poke people who I would not be able to reach with only my arms. I can pick up a rock and hurl it at a wolf that is still some distance away. I can set up a device such that, if I press a button, something terrible will happen to intruders in the woods. That is, our epistemological reach can extend beyond our capacity for action, and our capacity for action can extend beyond our epistemological reach.

One obvious way in which we can extend our epistemological reach further into the world than even our eyes will allow is for information about what is happening or has happened in other places to be reported to us by people who were there at the time. That is, someone could come in and tell me that yesterday he or she had seen half-a-dozen wolves running down the path a mile from my cave; something I could not have seen myself from where I am standing. I shall call what I am told or shown 'a representation' and I shall sometimes speak of us as being in a 'representation relation' to states of affairs.

The difference between a confrontation relation and a representation relation aligns with the difference between situations in which our mental states are online and situations in which our mental states are offline. That is, in confrontation relations our mental states are caused by perceptual inputs from the objects of those states, and which cause actions towards objects in our egocentric space. In representation relations our mental states are not caused by perceptions of the objects of those states, and do not result in actions towards objects in our egocentric space (although, of course, they can still cause actions). We could say, although it hardly needs saying, that acting on objects not in our egocentric space is not possible because we have no instrumental beliefs (we could have no instrumental beliefs) that could make it possible. When I talk about action, I shall, unless I qualify it, mean action directed upon objects in our egocentric space.

It might be objected that I am simply equivocating on the term 'possible'. Once that equivocation is sorted out, the distinction between non-fictional and fictional representations is reinstated as fundamental. It is possible (we could have instrumental beliefs) that we can act towards the objects in non-fictional representations. Difficult as it might be, we could track down and help the suffering victim seen on the news. It is not possible (we could not have instrumental beliefs) that we could act towards the objects in fictional representations. We could not track down and help the suffering children in Dotheboys Hall. However, all this does is reinforce the point. If it is possible for us to act we are in a confrontation relation with the object of our action. All this shows is that it might be unclear at the outset whether a representation relation could be turned into a confrontation relation. Representation relations which cannot will include all fictional representations and also all non-fictional representations where we lack instrumental beliefs that would enable us to act: that is, all non-fictional representations that are out of our grasp because they are separated in time, in space, or both.

Producing and understanding representations is like any other ability, for example, like the ability to run.[5] There are many functions that running can play in our lives. We can run to get somewhere quickly, we can run to get away from something. We can run to get fit, or we can run for pleasure. We can run and not get anywhere at all—on a treadmill at the gym. However, it is all simply running and if we want an account of running it will need to be neutral between these different functions. Similarly, there is the human ability to construct and understand representations. This might have the function of saying what has happened or is happening elsewhere (news) or saying what happened a long time ago (history). In addition, I will argue, we can extend the account somewhat. Representations can include speculation of what could happen or what might have happened at some other place or (an inclusive 'or') some other time: hypotheses and suppositions, thought experiments, and, ultimately, fiction. However, it is all simply producing and understanding representations and an account of representations will be neutral between these different functions. This is not to say, of course, that the differences between the functions might not be important. Similarly, differences between the functions of running might be important: if one is running to get away from a wolf one does not want to be on a treadmill. My claim is that such differences, in the case of representations, need to be sorted out further down the line after we have an account of understanding representations as such.

Given what I have said, what would we expect representations to be like? Let us focus on the simple role outlined above of extending our epistemological reach by telling us of things that have happened at some other time or place. That is, the representation needs to convey information, and it needs to convey it in a form that will be useful to us. We need to be told what is going on in a way that will help us were the same sort of thing to start going on in our environment. The information has to be given in such a way that is generalizable: we need news of events, and reasons or explanations of those events. It looks as if we need what philosophers have discussed under the title of 'narrative'.

---

[5] For the view that representations are ubiquitous in our lives, see Schank and Berman 2002 and Lamarque and Olsen 1994: ch. 9.

Noel Carroll has given the following definition of 'the narrative connection':

> A narrative connection obtains when (1) the discourse represents at least two events and/or states of affairs (2) in a globally unified forward-looking manner (3) concerning the career of at least one unified subject (4) where the temporal relations between the events and/or states of affairs are perspicuously ordered, and (5) where the earlier events in the sequence are at least causally necessary conditions for the causation of later events and/or states of affairs (or are contributions thereto). (Carroll 2000: 126)

Narrative form is a particularly appropriate way to relate events that have happened in some other time and place in that it is potentially richly informative. Events are described, along with the connections between the events, in a way that is easily generalizable. It could be argued that narratives are not the only form a representation can take: a collage of facts and impressions might, on some occasion, be a better vehicle. This seems a difficult matter to decide. The form in which an account is given (which may be a collage) might not be the form in which it is understood (it may be ordered by the listener into a narrative). Although I am not making the strong claim that only narratives can represent, I shall focus on narrative representations in what follows. This is partly because they are a particularly powerful form of representation, and partly because the psychology of text processing (which I will discuss in Chapters 5 and 6) is couched in terms of understanding narratives.

Although the examples that Carroll and others in this debate use are exclusively of past events, nothing in the definition rules out narratives that tell of events that are happening simultaneously with the telling. It is important that my epistemological grasp is able to extend to events happening now as much as to events happening in the past. That is, it is as useful for me to know what is happening to the wolf that has just run into the cave next door as it would be for me to know what happened when the wolf ran into a cave last week. The story of a cricket match that unfolds as the commentator describes, in the ball-by-ball commentary, what is happening on the field is a narrative as it unfolds; it does not only become a narrative once the match has ended.

Philosophical debate on definitions such as that by Carroll has centred on whether (5) is necessary. Currie discusses a case (first bought forward by David Velleman) of a story related by Aristotle: 'Mitys was murdered, and the murderer of Mitys went on to be killed by a falling statue of Mitys himself' (Currie 2010: 29).[6] Here the two key events are not causally connected, and yet we seem intuitively to have a narrative. Currie has suggested a way forward, which is that we give up trying to divide representations into two sorts, narrative and non-narrative, and instead think of grading representations according to their degrees of narrativity (Currie 2010: 33–6). A representation is high in narrativity when it is high in features characteristic of narrative. As Currie argues, this has the additional advantage of reflecting the context-dependence of our classifications of something as a narrative. We might want to distinguish a parable from a novel by claiming the former is not a narrative (a parable simply draws general conclusions from the particular) but distinguish both a parable and a novel from 'something so unnarrative-like as mathematical physics' by claiming both the former are narratives (Currie 2010: 35).

I claimed above that representations are 'information about what is happening or has happened in other places'. My stipulation of what it is to be a representation is narrower than some. Mathematical physics, recipes, instruction manuals and the like will not be representations. That is, generally they will not be; some might contain episodes that provide information about what has happened elsewhere. In such cases, at least part of them is a representation and—I shall assume—that part of them will possess a degree of narrativity.

The conclusion to which this chapter has been working is that the distinction between confrontations and representations is more fundamental than the distinction between non-fictions and fictions. Confrontations do not require the imagination; I do not need to imagine being confronted by a wolf if there is one before me. Something is needed to explain my engagement with representations, whether that is through *de se* imagining or making them vivid to ourselves. If philosophy does need some notion of a DCA or 'make-believe', it applies to this category rather than only to fictions. This notion of 'engagement' breaks up into a number of different problems. First, there are issues to do with causation: it is clear why being in a confrontation relation with a wolf should grab our interest, but why should being in a representation relation with a wolf? Also, nothing much needs to be said regarding our being caused to feel fear when confronted

---

[6] The Velleman discussion can be found in Velleman 2003. The original can be found in the *Poetics*, 1452a4–6.

by a wolf, while something needs to be said about being caused to fear when faced with a representation of a wolf or even being caused to fear for a represented person being stalked by a represented wolf. Second, there are constitutive issues. No account is needed of my being engaged with things that I confront. What, however, is the account of my being engaged with representations? After all, I cannot interact with them; they are distant from me by being in a different space or by happening at a different time or by not being spatially or temporally related to me at all. There are, in addition, more specific issues: confronted with a wolf, I believe I am in grave danger and feel threatened and terrified. However, confronted with a representation of a wolf, I do not believe I am in grave danger, yet, in some circumstances, it appears to me to that I feel threatened and terrified. How can this be? As Walton says (I have already quoted this in Chapter 2) 'What is pity or anger which is never to be acted on? What is love that cannot be expressed to its object and it logically or metaphysically incapable of consummation?' (Walton 1990: 196). What is the correct account of these mental states? To anticipate, I am unconvinced that there is a role for the imagination in answering these questions. Shorn of the need to accommodate fiction, we can see that basically what is needed is an account of *understanding* narrative. *The extent to which such an account need make use of the imagination is an entirely open question.* Until we have found a role for the imagination, the jury remains out on the question of the continued viability of the philosophical industry on make-believe.

Ditching the distinction between non-fiction and fiction in favour of the distinction between confrontations and representations does not only question the relevance of work on the imagination but on the philosophy of fiction more generally. The contrast is particularly stark when set against the position of Peter Lamarque and Stein Haugom Olsen. Their position is built around two key claims. The first is that the division between non-fiction and fiction is fundamental.

The truth is that the classification of narrative into fiction and non-fiction is of the utmost significance; not only is it a precondition of making sense of a work, but it determines how we should respond both in thought and action. (Lamarque and Olsen 1994: 30)

The second is that fiction is defined by 'the fictive stance':

The fictive story-teller, making up a story, makes and presents sentences (or propositions, i.e. sentence-meanings) for a particular kind of attention. The aim, at first approximation, is this:

for the audience to make-believe (imagine or pretend) that the standard speech act commitments associated with the sentences are operative even while knowing they are not.

Attending to the sentences in this way is to adopt the *fictive stance* towards them. (Lamarque and Olsen 1994: 43)

My view denies both of these claims.

Let me assume (rather optimistically) that the consensus view has accepted the cogency of my arguments. Holders of the view might concede that they have failed to make the case for a propositional attitude necessary to explain our engaging with fictions. However, they might still hold on to the link between imagination and 'perspective shifting' and maintain that 'the imagination' is the correct way to describe our engaging with representations (whether non-fictional or fictional). There seem to me advantages and disadvantages with this position. The advantages are that one can use the valuable work done by Walton, Currie, and others to elucidate our engaging with representations. However, there are also disadvantages.[7] I will mention four.

First, the obvious one, using the term 'imagination' encourages us to think that there is something about the exercise of our imaginations that links it exclusively to fiction rather than representations generally, whether non-fiction or fiction. This is particularly so if we switch to another term common in the literature, which is synonymous with the imagination, namely, 'make-believe'. The purported advantage with the term 'make-believe' is that it can be used without strain as the description of a mental state (we make-believe that p) and an operator on propositions (it is make-believe that p).[8] The first is simply another way of picking out the mental state of 'imagining that p' and the second picks out those propositions that are true-in-fiction and not true *simpliciter*. It is then easy to slip into thinking that the latter form the content of the former: that is, we make-believe those propositions that are make-believe. Rather than being a trivial truth, we can see now that this is a substantial, and false, claim. The propositions that we make-believe would not include those that are the content of any fiction (only thick fiction) and would include many propositions that are not make-believe: the content of all thick non-fictions and

[7] Those who hold the consensus view should notice that nowhere, in the thousands of pages of the psychology of text processing I have read (which incorporates processing both non-fictional and fictional representations) is there mention of 'the imagination'.

[8] See Currie 1990: 72. Currie does not make the mistake identified below, although, as we saw above, he links the imagination specifically to fiction, not to thick representations.

the content of all thick fictions that are also true. To think that we can switch between 'make-believe' as a mental state and 'make-believe' as an operator on propositions without substantially changing what we are talking about would be to confuse engaging with fictions with engaging with representations more generally.

Second, using 'imagination' as the term to describe the mental state of those engaged with thick representations obviates an important distinction. Consider the following passage from *King Lear*, where Edgar is trying to convince the blind Gloucester that he is standing on the edge of a cliff.

> Come on, sir; here's the place: stand still. How fearful
> And dizzy 'tis, to cast one's eyes so low!
> The crows and choughs that wing the midway air
> Show scarce so gross as beetles: half way down
> Hangs one that gathers samphire, dreadful trade!
> Methinks he seems no bigger than his head:
> The fishermen, that walk upon the beach,
> Appear like mice; and yond tall anchoring bark,
> Diminish'd to her cock; her cock, a buoy
> Almost too small for sight: the murmuring surge,
> That on the unnumber'd idle pebbles chafes,
> Cannot be heard so high. I'll look no more;
> Lest my brain turn, and the deficient sight
> Topple down headlong.
>
> (*King Lear*, Act IV, Scene VI)

We can, when we read this, recreate the sights and sounds in the imagination (I shall qualify this claim in Chapter 5). Readers might pause on this passage to visualize the scene described and imagine hearing the chafing of the unnumbered pebbles. However, this is a quite particular task; not part of the usual engagement with the text. In other words, there are two distinct experiences here. First, there is the experience of engaging with the representation. Second, there is the experience of exercising the imagination as a result of engaging with the representation. This seems a worthwhile distinction, and one way of marking it would be to reserve the term 'imagination' for the latter. This is not to say that the consensus view lacks the resources to make this distinction; they do not. They could describe what I have called 'engaging with the representation' using the propositional imagination, while the richer experiential state will draw on other aspects of the imagination: both the visual and the aural imagination.

The third disadvantage concerns the relation between our interaction with thin narratives (which do not require the imagination) and thick narratives (which do). That is, with thin narratives we have the usual mechanisms of processing beliefs. With thick narratives we have a new mental state: the imagination. What happens at the boundary? The point can be put in conceptual terms. At what point, and why, we do need to start reconceptualizing our mental states as imagination rather than belief? In addition, there is the question of the mechanisms of the mind; are new mental mechanisms called into play? If so, when and why? It is a methodological truism in the psychology of text processing that understanding fictional narratives and understanding non-fictional narratives employ the same cognitive processes (Gerrig 1993: 7; Bortolussi and Dixon 2003: 117; Worth 2004). Furthermore, if we shift one step down to the evidence from neuroscience, Timothy Schroeder and Carl Matheson have reviewed the evidence and concluded that 'insofar as the imagination causes the same feelings as the real, it does so by using the same structures in the brain as those used by the real world' (Schroeder and Matheson 2006: 30). The fact that the underlying psychological and neurophysiological mechanisms are the same does not entail that folk-psychological accounts of engagement with non-fiction and fictional representations must be the same. However, it does raise the question as to whether we have got the folk psychology right, and whether there might not be a different way of conceptualizing matters that keeps the levels more sensibly aligned.

The fourth drawback (related to the third) concerns the level of psychological explanation at which the consensus view is pitched. According to Walton, when reading a thick representation the sentences on the page serve as props in a game of make-believe, which mandate us to imagine certain propositions. I read 'Elinor drew near, but without saying a word; and seated herself on the bed, took her hand, kissed her affectionately several times, and then gave way to a burst of tears, which as first was scarcely less violent than Marianne's' (Austen 1975: 145). This mandates me to imagine that p, where p is the proposition that sentence expresses. This, in turn can lead to further experiences: imagining that Marianne is unhappy can lead to imagining Marianne's unhappiness, which can arouse a state describable within the 'game' of our engagement with *Sense and Sensibility* as 'pity for Marianne' (Walton 1990: 353, 43, 245).

What is the state of 'imagining that p'? We have some grasp of the attitude of propositional imagining. It is not merely entertaining a proposition; to quote Walton again, 'Imagining (propositional imagining), like (propositional) believing or desiring, is doing something with a proposition one has in mind' (Walton 1990: 20). This seems part of our folk-psychological grasp of our concept of propositional imagining. However, in other places Walton stretches the concept. Consider the cornerstone of Walton's theory: 'It is the function, in any reasonable sense of the term, of ordinary representational works of art to serve as props in games of make-believe' (Walton 1990: 53). Now consider the obvious and rather blunt criticism of this theory. Anyone who is playing a game of make-believe knows that they are playing a game of make-believe. The average appreciator of a work of art does not know they are playing a game of make-believe, hence the average appreciator of a work of art is not playing a game of make-believe. Walton's reply here is that appreciators of works of art *implicitly accept* the principles of make-believe.

Insofar as it is the object's recognized function to be a prop in certain kinds of games, the principles are likely to seem natural, to be accepted automatically, to be internalized, and the prescribed imaginings are likely to occur spontaneously. (Walton 1990: 53, 246)

However, one might think that our folk psychology has it that playing games of make-believe is essentially a self-conscious activity; it cannot be done implicitly (Neill 1991). This raises the question—and no more than that, as I do not think any of these drawbacks are decisive against the consensus view—as to whether 'the imagination' is being used as a name for a process that is part of the *explanation* of our experience of representations. If so, then we need to look at how the consensus view, which is course-grained and high level, stands to the detailed accounts of what is going on in a reader's head.

This is the task of the next two chapters. I have argued that engaging with narratives (what we *do* with the propositions) is neutral between non-fictional and fictional narratives. It is time to put some more flesh on the bones, by examining the details of how readers use representations to construct mental models. I have appealed to work in psychology, partly because it provides this detail, partly because it accounts for non-fictional and fictional narratives, and partly because it provides the alternative we need to talk of the imagination.

5

Understanding Narratives

The psychological literature on text comprehension is vast. The proponents of each theory, account, or model, attempt to support their position with a wealth of empirical evidence garnered from increasingly complicated empirical tests on readers. It is not my intention to go through this literature passing judgement on what works and what does not; I do not possess the right skills, nor would it serve my purposes. Instead, I will outline and discuss some of the conclusions, and draw out the consequences they have for a philosophical account of reading. I shall begin by laying out some of the areas of interest, elements, and methodological assumptions of the discipline before looking at the conclusions that have emerged.

There are broadly three areas of interest. The first is looking at the processing of reading itself; that is, the cognitive processes that actually happen during reading. The second is looking at the nature of the mental representation that results from reading. The third is looking at the relations between such mental representations and existing memory structures. I shall look at these over the next three chapters. I shall draw some further consequences for the philosophy of fiction in the two chapters after that.

Psychologists use the usual barrage of psychological resources, which—again—I shall divide into three. The first are predictions about what might happen in one situation generated by theories, models, and hypotheses tested in other situations. The second are 'verbal reports'; that is, 'the reader expresses ideas that come to mind as each clause in the text is comprehended'. The third—the most important set of measures—are behavioural measures that assess processing time. These include eye-tracking techniques and probing techniques such as measuring the time it takes for readers to bring to mind certain words, or remember certain incidents. I am indebted here to Graesser, Millis et al. (1997: 167).

Here is an illustrative example of the use of the three resources. In this example, Arthur Graesser and his colleagues report of attempts to find out whether readers of a simple narrative have in mind any or all of various goals of the characters, various parts of the causal sequence, and various other factors that are present. They begin with the narrative which they ask their subjects to read.

Once there was a Czar who had three lovely daughters. One day the three daughters went walking in the woods. They were enjoying themselves so much that they forgot the time and stayed too long. A dragon kidnapped the three daughters. As they were being dragged off they cried for help. Three heroes heard their cries and set off to rescue the daughters. The heroes came and fought the dragon and rescued the maidens. Then the heroes returned the daughters to their palace. When the Czar heard of the rescue, he rewarded the heroes.
Inferences when comprehending 'The dragon kidnapped the daughters':
1. Superordinate goal: The dragon wanted to eat the daughters.
2. Subordinate goal: The dragon grabbed the daughters.
3. Causal antecedent: The dragon saw the daughters.
4. Causal consequence: Someone rescued the daughters.
5. State: The dragon has scales. (Graesser, Singer et al. 1994: 389)

Different models or theories of text processing differ in their predictions as to which of the sorts of inference readers will encode. Hence, Graesser and his colleagues were able to test these predictions to produce evidence that will either count for or against those models or theories. The evidence is gathered using verbal reports and latency tests.

[Verbal reports] involved the collection of question-answering protocols while readers comprehended the stories clause by clause. After reading each clause (that referred to an action, event, or state), the subjects answered questions about the clause. One group answered a why-question, a second group answered a how-question, and a third group answered a what-happened-next question ... [In latency tests] a test word was presented 500 ms after each sentence in a story was read. The subjects were instructed to say the test word aloud as quickly as possible. The test word was sometimes a word that came from a superordinate goal and sometimes a word from a subordinate goal/action. These items were new inferences constructed for the first time in the story by explicit target actions. There also was a control condition in which the superordinate and subordinate inferences were named in an unrelated passage context. (Graesser, Singer et al. 1994: 389–90)

One might have doubts about the efficacy of the methodology of verbal reports. Thick representations bring their content into our attentional environment; reading *Sense and Sensibility* brings Barton Cottage to us, so we become oblivious to our vulgar surroundings and the passing of time. If the task is to form a psychological account of this phenomenon, it is unclear that using verbal reports that drag the reader out of Barton Cottage to ask them questions is the right way to do so. In response to this, psychologists tend not to rely on verbal reports alone, but put that evidence alongside evidence from other sources.[1]

In addition to the three approaches for eliciting data, text processing relies on three elements: information sources, memory stores and levels of representation. I will take each in turn.

The information sources are the text itself, the background knowledge of the reader, and a catch-all category of 'context' or 'strategy'. As we are attempting to give a theory of understanding, we should not regard 'the text' as a string of uninterpreted symbols. I am not concerned with the process that takes us from marks on the page to words so will regard the text as the input in whatever form from the page into our cognitive processing system.

'The background knowledge of the reader' is a broad category, which can be divided into a number of different sorts. The first sort is basically language skill, which is part of 'bottom up' processing. This will vary from the very basic (understanding language) up through levels of complexity: the ability to keep track of pronouns, tracking spatial and temporal continuities, causal connections and motivational continuities, and the ability to note examples of incoherence. It is a moot point (as we shall find out) whether other skills are involved. In addition, at a higher level of complexity, there is 'top down' processing. Readers can draw on general schemata (also known as 'frames' or 'scripts') to fill in the gaps between what is given in the text. For example, a writer does not need to go into exhaustive details in describing two characters entering a restaurant and eating a meal. From their prior knowledge of restaurants, readers are able to activate their 'restaurant schema' and fill in details such

---

[1] Having made the point, there is evidence for the reliability of verbal reports: 'Researchers have satisfactorily demonstrated that particular classes inferences exposed by verbal protocols do in fact predict these on-line temporal measures collected from different groups of readers…These studies have shown that some, but not all, classes of inference from the verbal protocols are generated online. Therefore, theories of interference generation can be tested by coordinating verbal protocol analyses and online temporal measures' (Graesser, Singer et al. 1994: 386). By 'on-line' inferences psychologists mean automatically encoded inferences; all other inferences made with respect to the reading are 'off-line'.

as that there will be a table, that there will be a waiter or waitress, that food will be eaten, that the meal will be paid for, and so on. In a series of experiments, Gordon Bower and his colleagues showed that, when readers attempted to recall a text they had read featuring some stereotypical situation (that is, some situation for which they would be expected to have a schema) they tended to recall events that would feature in their schema, but did not explicitly feature in the texts. Furthermore, if the text placed events in a different order to that of the schema, readers tended to recall the events as they would feature in the schema, rather than how they did feature in the text. Furthermore, when, further on in the text, one of the characters has a tomato stain on their shirt or claims not to be hungry the reader can infer that this came about as a result of the visit to the restaurant (Bower, Black et al. 1979; see also Owens, Bower et al. 1979).

'Background knowledge' can also be meant in a more literal sense; that is, as akin to 'specialist knowledge'. Consider, for example, the following paragraph of cricket commentary:

Capes hammers another straight-driven maximum off Afridi, so effortless, like picking grapes off the belly of a supermodel. Trott attempts a very risky reverse sweep, but only an underside edge prevents his wicket from being castled. Bit unnecessary, especially with Pietersen batting like a Jedi. Use the Fours. (Test Match Special commentary, retrieved 11 February 2010).

This is likely to be largely incomprehensible to those without a knowledge of cricket—and possibly even a knowledge of the conventions of Test Match Special, not to mention *Star Wars*. This too has been the subject of experiments in psychology concluding, unsurprisingly, that prior knowledge not only facilitates recall of texts, but also directs reader's attention to the relevant issues in the text (Gerrig 1993: 41).[2]

Like 'background knowledge,' 'context' or 'strategy' also covers a wide range. It could refer to the context in which the representation is encountered; our processing of a text (the attention we pay, what we pick up as salient) may well differ between our hearing a news report or our hearing

---

[2] Intriguingly, the relationship between background knowledge and the ability to recall the content of a text is not always linear. Readers with intermediate knowledge can sometimes recall more than both those with low knowledge and experts. This is thought to be because of differences in the way that experts' prior knowledge is organised (Magliano, Zwaan et al. 1999).

a fisherman's tale of the one that got away (I shall say a little about this in the next chapter under the subject of genre) (van Dijk 1999). It also refers to what researchers take to be the purpose of reading the text. I shall say something about this presently.

The memory stores, which turn out to be illuminating in considering the experience of reading, are divided into three. There is the short-term memory ('STM'), which is very limited; often thought to hold only the most recent clause that has been read. The working memory ('WM') is slightly larger, holding approximately the last two sentences plus any information that the text is prompting the reader to recall or recycle. Finally, there is the long-term memory (LTM) which is everything else including any memories of what has been previously recounted in the text, as well as memory structures that were in place before the reader began to read the text.

The number of levels of representation proposed is a function of how fine-grained is the psychological explanation. Most make use of at least two: the 'textbase' and the 'situation model' (van Dijk and Kintsch 1983). The textbase is the gist of the text; its semantic content and structure. The situation model is a representation of the state of affairs described by the text. This is more familiar to philosophers as a 'mental model'. As I am not particularly interested in the details of the psychological machinery, I shall ignore representation at the textbase level and instead consider features of the mental model. Here is a more detailed description of such by Philip Johnson-Laird:

… mental models play a central and unifying role in representing objects, states of affairs, sequences of events, the way the world is, and the social and psychological actions of daily life. They enable individuals to make inferences and predictions, to understand phenomena, to decide what action to take to control its execution, and above all to experience events by proxy; they allow language to be used to create representations comparable to those deriving from direct acquaintance with the world; and they relate word to the world by way of conception and perception. (Johnson-Laird 1983: 397)

The general schema is this. When engaging with a representation, we draw on our information sources (the text, our background knowledge, modified by context and our goals), using our various memories, to construct the mental model.

There are at least two ways in which the concerns of the psychologists do not align neatly with the concerns of philosophers. First, there is the question of the artificiality of the text to be processed (the text used in the example above, in comparison to most, is relatively rich). These texts, usually written by the psychologists themselves with an eye for the experiment they want to undertake, are devoid of interesting plot and literary merit. The reason for this is summed up in a book that provides an overview of the area.

> Most of the analysis and research…is based on the assumption that readers have the goal of identifying the apparent point or message of the narrator. Our justification for the focus on this one goal is that it is likely to be salient for most readers most of the time. (Bortolussi and Dixon 2003: 243)

There is surely something to this, in that 'identifying the apparent point or message' is basic for whatever strategy a reader might have. However, the assumption limits the scope of the conclusions. Reading subjects tend to be undergraduates, and psychology allows for, rather than foregrounds, the fact that the critical reading of literature is a skill that it may take many years and much effort to develop. The difference between engaging with a thin representation and engaging with a thick representation is generally ignored. In what follows we need to be wary of generalizing; what is true of an unskilled reader following a simple plot might not be true of a skilled reader coming to terms with Joseph Conrad or Henry James.

As stated above, the 'purpose of reading a text', which includes having a more than shallow interest in the text, comes under the heading of a reader's 'strategy'. Psychology tends to focus on the simplest case: reading merely for understanding of a realistic narrative. However, oddly, shortly before the passage quoted above the authors spell out reading goals in more detail, which sound a great deal more sophisticated.

> Generally we assume that readers do not read narratives for any one purpose. Rather, we imagine that a hierarchy of goals is relevant at any one time. These might include, for example, the aesthetic appreciation of the language of the narrative, an understanding of the events of the story world, an evaluation of the mental state of the narrator or characters, and appreciation of relations among characters or between characters and institutions, and an interpretation of the point or theme of the implied author. (Bortolussi and Dixon 2003: 242–43)

These goals argue for a richer engagement with the text than simply 'identifying the apparent point or message'. This is something we need to bear in mind in what follows.

The second failure of alignment between psychology and philosophy is that psychology tends to limit itself to tracking what happens between our reading the text, tracking the various relations, and constructing the mental model. It is generally presupposed that the relations unfold as the text unfolds; in the example above, the text provides the information in the same sequence as the events described occur: first the daughters walk in the woods, then the dragon kidnaps them, then the heroes fight the dragon, and then the heroes are rewarded. However, the sequence of events *as* reported need not follow the sequence of events reported. That is, psychology tends to ignore the distinction between 'discourse' and 'story': 'Discourse' refers to the unfolding of events in the narrative, 'story' refers to the sequence of events that constitute the plot (Chatman 1990: 9). Thus, the narrative above could have started with the heroes being rewarded, and then had a 'flashback' to the walk in the woods and the events that followed. In such a case the sequence in which the reader encounters the events in the discourse would not match the sequence of events in the story. To accommodate this, readers need to monitor several sorts of continuity, and react to discontinuities where they occur. This complicates matters, but not in a way that undermines the whole project (see Zwaan, Langston et al. 1995; Magliano, Zwaan et al. 1999).

Having dealt with the preliminaries, let us attempt to draw something out of the work. The question at issue is the extent of the construction readers form as a result of engaging with a text: in other words, how rich is the mental model which results? The obvious methodology is to examine the nature of the processing that happens when we engage with a representation, to start from what happens automatically (that is, the bare minimum of what goes on) and see how far we need to expand from there. Gail McKoon and Roger Ratcliffe argue for what they call 'the minimalist hypothesis'. That is, 'that the only inferences that are automatically encoded when reading are those that are easily available, and those that are necessary for local coherence' (McKoon and Ratcliff 1992). Let us look at each of these in turn. By 'automatically encoded,' McKoon and Ratcliffe mean 'those that are encoded in the absence of special goals or strategies on the part of the reader, and they are constructed in the first few hundred milliseconds of processing'. By 'easily available', they mean 'well-known information from general knowledge and explicit information from the

text being read'. 'Local coherence' is a little more complicated. McKoon
and Ratcliffe are explicit by what they mean by 'local':

> *Local coherence* is defined for those propositions of a text that are in working mem-
> ory at the same time; in other words, propositions that are no farther apart in the
> text than one or two sentences. Many of the inferences that establish local coher-
> ence are based on information that is easily available because it is in short-term
> memory. (McKoon and Ratcliff 1992: 441).

They do not go into much detail as to what it is that underpins 'coherence'.
This is unfortunate, as 'coherence' will differ with different genres of text.
Being in two places at once might not be a local incoherence in a tale about
Harry Potter and his friends but would be in a biography of the Duke of
Wellington (I explore these issues in Chapter 9). McKoon and Ratcliffe say
that coherence includes 'connections among instances of the same concept,
pronominal reference and perhaps causal relations'. They also include inferences among concepts—for example, readers could infer that 'dog' and 'col-
lie' referred to the same animal (McKoon and Ratcliff 1992: 441). They also
speculate that 'bridging inferences'—that is, the inference that two different referring expressions pick out the same item—might be encoded. For
example, readers were given the following text to read 'Police are hunting
a man in hiding. The wife of Bob Birch disclosed illegal business practices
in an interview on Sunday.' A sub-group of the readers were also given a
sentence that made the inference (that Bob Birch was the man in hiding)
explicit. The fact that both sets of readers took equal lengths of time to agree
to the claim 'Bob Birch was the man in hiding' suggests that the bridging
inference was encoded in the first case (McKoon and Ratcliff 1992: 444).

One of the most discussed issues in the text processing literature concerns the extent to which causal relations are encoded. According to
McKoon and Ratcliffe, the only causal relations that are encoded are those
that are readily available and those required for local coherence. Intuitively,
one might think that readers might keep in mind the overarching goals of
a character: that he or she is in search of a lost treasure, or trying to build a
coalition for government. The evidence is that this is not the case; readers
follow the text as they read, with the overall rationale for the characters'
actions being put to one side. More indicative of the gaps in the mental
models is that readers do not make inferences about how actions were per-
formed. The text might tell us that characters ate their food, yet the readers
did not assign the instruments by which they ate their food (presumably, a

knife and fork) to the mental model. Finally, predictions based on extrapolating causation are also seldom assigned to the model; the only circumstances in which they are assigned is when there is something explicit in the text that prompts the reader to look forward. The text might say 'The actress jumped from the window and fell fourteen floors onto the concrete,' but tests show that, unless prompted, readers do not encode the proposition that the actress is dead (McKoon and Ratcliff 1992: 442).

This might all seem rather vague. However, as things turn out, that does not matter for, as we shall see, these divisions are more an argumentative convenience than a psychological reality. The most prominent rival to the minimalist hypothesis is 'constructivism'. McKoon and Ratcliffe construe constructivism as the rather extravagant hypothesis that encoding depends on 'whether an inference is required for a lifelike description of the event described by the text' (McKoon and Ratcliff 1992: 456). Proponents of constructivism are more cautious:

The constructionist theory assumes that readers encode three sets of inferences, namely (*a*) inferences that address the readers' comprehension goals, (*b*) inferences that explain *why* events, actions, and states occur, and (*c*) inferences that establish coherence in the situation model at local and global levels. (Graesser, Millis et al. 1997: 182)

The minimalists take the evidence of their experiments to show that— 'in the absence of special goals or strategies'—only those inferences that are either easily available or needed for local coherence are automatically encoded. The constructivists claim that their evidence shows that readers also automatically encode inferences required for global coherence—that is, coherence over more than that available in the working memory. Both minimalists and constructivists agree that the 'special goals or strategies' of the reader will make a difference to the inferences they encode. For example, if a subject reads a text describing a walk through a house, knowing that they are going to face questions as to what is in the rooms of the house, then they will rehearse the content of those rooms as they read (McKoon and Ratcliff 1992: 459). Indeed, there is continuum between reading for comprehension—the 'automatic processing'—and a host of other ways we might have for engaging with a text. One can already see that the clash between the two positions might be more apparent than real in that the minimalist explicitly excludes, and the constructivist includes, consideration of 'the readers' comprehension goals'. Furthermore, the minimalists allow that global inferences are made if reader's goals require it or if local coherence breaks down, and also that some global inferences are partially encoded (McKoon and Ratcliff 1992: 445, 458). Indeed, both McKoon and Ratcliffe for the minimalists and Graesser and colleagues for the constructivists admit that their differences might be more differences in emphasis rather than of kind.

The textbase position and minimalist hypotheses are probably correct when the reader is very quickly reading the text, when the text lacks global coherence, and when the reader has very little background knowledge. The constructionist theory is on the mark when the reader is attempting to comprehend the text for enjoyment or mastery at a more leisurely pace, when the text has global coherence, and when the reader has some background knowledge. (Graesser, Millis et al. 1997: 183). (See also McKoon and Ratcliff 1992: 463; Graesser, Singer et al. 1994: 372).

As we have seen, even constructivism will be too minimal when it comes to processing more complicated texts; that is, those in which the sequence of events in the discourse is different to the sequence of events in the story. There, readers will operate according to an 'event indexing' model:

The model assumes that readers simultaneously monitor continuities in story characters and objects, time, space, causality and intentionality. When a focal sentence describes an event that is continuous with respect to these situational dimensions, there is a high correspondence between the discourse structure and the story structure. However, discontinuities along these dimensions often occur when there are discrepancies between the discourse and story structures. It is under these conditions that readers must engage in effortful processing to construct a representation of the story structure. (Magliano, Zwaan et al. 1999: 222)

The nature of such 'effortful processing' is revealed, in part, by the interpretation of the results of the experiments designed to test it (see also (Rinck and Weber 2003)). It seems clear that rather than there being one mental structure at one node (of which more in the next chapter), readers will need several substructures which they integrate as they go along (Magliano, Zwaan et al. 1999: 242).

The 'as they go along' is important, as representations in which the discourse and story are radically distinct require a different treatment. Consider Ambrose Bierce's short story, 'An Occurrence at Owl Creek Bridge'.[3] In this, a Confederate sympathizer, Peyton Farquhar is about to be

---

[3] Nick Diehl introduced me to this story, and made clear to me its importance to the philosophy of narrative.

hanged. At the last moment, the rope snaps and he falls into the river. His experience is lucid, almost hallucinatory. He climbs out of the river, and, driven on by thoughts of his family, finds his way home. On arrival, he is about to greet his lovely wife when there is a flash, his neck snaps, and we are left to conclude that what we have been reading is a narrative of what was going through his mind in the second between him being pushed off the bridge and his neck breaking. In this case, it is appropriate for the reader to construct the mental model which represents Farquhar's journey home. The twist at the end does not require that we change the model; it only requires that we cease to believe that the contents of the representation (that is, the contents of the model) describe a journey home, but rather describe what went on in Farquar's imagination as he was hanged. We construct the model of the journey home in order to learn about what was going on in his imagination. This is similar to Walton's solution to the problem of 'seeing the unseen'. If a visual representation mandates us to imagine seeing a scene which is in fact unseen (for example, a dinosaur roaming around) then we imagine seeing the dinosaur; the point of doing so is to learn what are to imagine exists unseen (Walton, 1990: 237–9). This similarity is not coincidental as the problems are, at root, the same.

The reader's experience does not, of course, stop at constructing a model of the states of affairs described in the text. There will also be readers' reactions to those states of affairs. These are non-inferential responses to the text, called by Richard Gerrig 'participatory responses' (or 'p-responses') (Gerrig, 1993: ch. 3). P-responses will cover a wide range of which this is only a rough taxonomy: problem solving 'with' the characters; wondering what they will do next or being in suspense about their situations; emotions felt for the characters such as feeling pity for the characters or cheering them on; emotions felt for ourselves such as feelings of excitement, hope, awe, and sadness; and an appreciation of the atmosphere of the work, such as its mood, and a sense of time or a sense of place. These are a rich and heterogeneous group, each category of which deserves a chapter to itself (some will appear in the discussion of the so-called 'paradox of fiction' in Chapter 8). However, as I would like to move on and discuss other matters, I shall only discuss two broad issues that pertain to them all: non-cognitive affect ('mood'), and how p-responses stand to consciousness.

The link between our being in a certain mood and what we recall, attend to, and judge is well established (Forgas and Bower 1987). A 'mood', in philosophy, has come to designate an affective state that lacks a cognitive component. Examples might be a generalized sadness and generalized anxiety. That is, one is not sad or anxious about anything; rather, one's sadness or anxiety is 'free-floating'. The claim is that a narrative might have certain properties that affect the reader's mood, which in turn affects that which a reader notices or does not notice. Here is an example, due to Noel Carroll.

The survey of Dorothy's home in Kansas in the opening pages of L. Frank Baum's *The Wizard of Oz* finds grayness everywhere. Grayness as a color or as a psychological state is mentioned ten times in six short paragraphs. Additionally, it is overtly contrasted with joy and fun. Other features of the place that are emphasized are its isolation; it is in the middle of vast prairies and the lumber for the house came from far away. It is parched—the grass is burnt-out and the paint blistered. The household itself is claustrophobic and cramped. Dorothy's guardians, Aunt Em and Uncle Henry, are described as austere—both are joyless, or, laughless, as gray mentally as the landscape is physically. (Carroll 2003: 536)

The fact that doleful properties are repeatedly mentioned does not entail that readers will feel doleful. However, as standard mood-induction technique in psychology is to ask subjects to read mood-inducing text, it is a reasonable assumption that it would. The reader will probably not notice the properties of the text that are acting on him or her (that is, not be aware of them acting); rather, the affective responses are automatic. Once the reader is in such an affective state, that will prime him or her to attend to certain properties (those in a positive mood tend to notice positive things) and foreground certain information. Amy Coplan has made the case for this being part of the regular armoury of film-makers. A particularly vivid example is the opening sequence of *Blade Runner* in which viewers see a cityscape of a dystopian Los Angeles, against the background of some atmospheric music by Vangelis (Coplan 2010). Coplan argues that this induces a mood that primes the viewers for the emotional roller coaster that is to come.

The issue of the relation between p-responses and consciousness raises the broader question of how much we can take to be going on in a reader's head at any one time. In respect of this, p-responses divide into two sorts: those that compete with the process of reading and those that do not. That is, when we read our minds are on the text and processing the text. Some of the p-responses could fit as part of this while others would seem to require that we stop reading in order to work through them. The basic division is between tasks in which differential attention is possible and tasks in which it is not.

Tasks in which differential attention is possible include the automatic responses we have, in particular, the arousal of emotion. In cases in which we are engrossed in the narrative, I suspect the usual case is that we experience the moods or emotions and yet we are not aware of them as they are happening (although we would be if we were particularly self-aware, and, even if we are not, we could become aware of them). It is a familiar experience, for example, to find oneself so gripped by an episode one barely notices time passing, and yet, in retrospect, one might describe oneself as being on the edge of one's seat or in a state of unbearable tension. Alternatively, one might close the book and find, to one's surprise, that tears have been running down one's cheeks. Reactions to representations can be similar to a more general experience of the emotions, here described by Peter Goldie.

You are driving a car and you see another car, out of control, approaching you on the wrong side of the road. You realise just what is going on, you see the danger to yourself and your passengers, and, with great speed and dexterity, you take the necessary evasive action. Then, when your car has finally come to a halt, you think with horror of just how close you were to death; your realize that you are bathed in a cold sweat, you see the whiteness of your knuckles as you still clench the steering wheel, and you feel your heart pumping. Looking back on the experience, you now agree that you were afraid whilst you were taking evasive action even though, you now can also say, you did not feel fear at the time. (Goldie 2000: 62)

The p-responses that seem incompatible with reading include those that require us to work things out, and also some instances of visualizing the scene described. Gerrig considers the first of these and concludes that certain p-responses will be rather sketchy.

[Problem-solving] p-responses will most likely not, under ordinary circumstances, come into consciousness in an explicit way. Most instances of this class of p-responses will emerge alongside the moment-to-moment experience of the narrative. They can be completely well formed only if the reader shifts attention fully away from the narrative—a practice that will be impractical if the narrative itself cannot be momentarily arrested (as will be the case for plays, conversational stories and so on). Even when the narrative is in printed form, the reader may not want to delay access to the desired knowledge by deliberately shifting attention to the activity of p-responding. Nonetheless, I suspect that most readers could catch themselves imagining at least ill-formed operations ('Perhaps he could . . .')

or offering themselves sketchy proofs ('I am sure she won't die because...') as part of the experience of narrative. (Gerrig 1993: 85)

The question of the compatibility of reading and visualizing has been the subject of empirical study. There is some controversy as to whether the compatibility consists of an 'overload' of a single channel of processing, or a 'bottleneck' in getting to that processing (Pashler and Johnston 1998). Whatever the mechanism, the evidence is that it is difficult to read about and visualize some state of affairs concurrently (Brooks 1967).

In looking at text-processing, we started with what McKoon and Ratcliffe call 'automatic encoding': 'those that are encoded in the absence of special goals or strategies on the part of the reader, and they are constructed in the first few hundred milliseconds of processing' (McKoon and Ratcliff 1992: 444). We have ended up talking about processes—problem-solving and visualizing—that seem additions to the basic strategy of reading for understanding. As we have seen with both problem-solving and visualizing, sketchy forms of them are compatible with reading. This suggests that we have a continuum here rather than a difference in kind, a view which chimes with at least some of the psychological literature (a reminder: by 'on-line' psychologists mean 'automatically encoded' and all other inferences the reader makes with respect to the text are 'off-line').

For the convenience of communication, we consider whether each class of inferences is in one of two discrete states: on-line versus off-line. However, there undoubtedly is a probabilistic continuum between on-line and off-line. The continuum can be attributed to fluctuations in reader abilities, reader goals, text materials, samples of inferences, experimental tasks, and so on. The continuum can also be explained by the theoretical possibility that inferences are encoded to some degree rather than all-or-none...The degree to which an inference is encoded might be strengthened or attenuated as more information is received. Technically speaking, when we claim that a class of inferences is generated on-line, our intention is to convey that it has a substantially higher strength of encoding or higher likelihood of being generated than the contrast classes of inferences that are off-line. A full-blown theory would account for likelihood of generation, the strength of encoding, the time-course of generation, and the exact locus of generation (within the text) for each class of inference. (Graesser, Singer et al. 1994: 376)

My interest is primarily in skilled readers engaging with complicated representations. The relevant question is whether engaging with representations such as histories, biographies, or novels involves readers in 'special goals or strategies'. There is no general answer to this question as there is no general biography or general novel. Different representations require different goals or strategies. One could speculate that some novels, 'airport novels' or stock page-turning thrillers, will be processed in much the same way as the little tale of the Czar and his lovely daughters. Other novels, for example, Anthony Powell's twelve novel sequence, *Dance to the Music of Time*, require a different strategy. The novels would be wasted on the reader who does not notice Powell's evocation of a sense of time and place, and who does not pause to recall where he or she has met a character before, what their relations are to the other characters, and how different characters can be formed regardless of similar backgrounds. Nonetheless, whatever the complex experience of the skilled reader, and whether we favour minimalism, constructivism, or the event-indexing model, the foregoing gives us some idea of what is goes on in our minds under our broad heading of 'imagination' or 'make-believe' (assuming these characterize our attitude to non-fictions and fictions). The consequence this has for a philosophical account of engaging with narrative is that it should make us cautious concerning claims as to what is involved in our imagining the content of the narrative. We can be misled by the rather rich accounts we find of mental models. Unless we have reason to think that the psychological processes of reading texts such as histories, biographies, and novels should differ completely from those that operate when reading the texts that feature in psychology experiments (a claim that would be empirically incredible) we have reason to think that the subsequent mental models are going to be rather vague and sketchy. In short, what goes on in our heads when we read is, generally, a great deal less exciting than we might have thought.

I shall conclude this chapter with a puzzle arising from the familiar complaint that, compared to engaging with books, engaging with films is imaginatively impoverished.

Without the elements of indeterminacy, the gaps in the texts, we should not be able to use our imagination. The truth of this observation is borne out by the experience many people have on seeing, for instance, the film of a novel. While reading *Tom Jones*, they may never have had a clear conception of what the hero actually looks like, but on seeing the film, some may say, 'That's not how I imagined him.' The point here is that the reader of *Tom Jones* is able to visualize the hero virtually for himself, and so his imagination senses the vast number of possibilities; the moment these possibilities are narrowed down to one complete and immutable picture, the imagination is put out of action, and we feel we have somehow been cheated. The may perhaps be an oversimplification of the process, but it does illustrate plainly the vital richness of potential that arises out of the fact that the hero in the novel must be pictured and cannot be seen. With the novel the reader must use his imagination to synthesize the information given him, and so his perception is simultaneously richer and more private; with the film he is confined merely to physical perception, and so whatever he remembers of the world he had pictured is brutally cancelled out. (Iser 1978: 283)

Apart from reminding us of the use to which the term 'imagination' was put prior to contemporary philosophy of fiction, this passage appears to raise a problem for my view. The fact that the reader, on seeing the film, says 'That's not how I imagined him' appears to entail that there was some way in which the reader *did* imagine him. Such detailed visualization would suggest, contrary to the view I favour, that the reader's mental model is rather rich. The entailment, however, does not hold (and neither does Iser take it to hold). Iser talks of the imagination sensing 'the vast number of possibilities' and 'the vital richness of potential'. Film narrows this down to 'one complete and immutable picture'. It is not that the reader has an image that competes with that provided in the film, but rather that the film resolves the imaginative play of the reader by providing a single image.

In the rest of the book, I will develop various themes that arise from this chapter. The next chapter returns to the claim that the most enlightening way of construing the debate is to provide a neutral account of understanding representations with other distinctions (such as the distinction between fiction and non-fiction) being sorted out elsewhere. Defending this claim requires accounting for that fact that what counts as local coherence in some fictional representations will differ from what counts as local coherence in other fictional or non-fictional representations. I will also provide further defence of the claim that the difference between fictional and non-fictional representations does not lie in their connection to action, in any simple connection to truth, or in any simple connection to our motivation for producing them or engaging with them. Chapter 7 looks at the vexed issue of the relation between our engagement with fiction and our structures of belief. Chapter 8 considers the (so-called) 'paradox of fiction,' while Chapter 9 attempts to dissolve the problems thought to arise with respect to fictional narrators, impossible fictions, as well as 'the fictionality puzzle' (a version of the (so-called) 'problem of imaginative resistance'). Finally, in Chapter 10 I will consider what my view entails for engaging with film. It should be clear already that how we process films will be very different from how we process written texts. Such differences will allow me to provide some defence of the traditional view (expressed above by Iser) that watching films really does not require much imagination.

6

Engaging with Narratives

The consensus view argues that the way in which we process non-fictional representations is different from the way in which we process fictional representations. That is, representations fall into two kinds: non-fiction and fiction. The propositions that form the content of the former kind have a systematically different relation to our pre-existing structures of belief than the propositions that form the content of the latter kind. As we have seen, a popular option is to hold that the former are dealt with by the usual Gricean mechanism that governs belief formation and the latter are dealt with by a Gricean mechanism that governs make-belief (or 'imagining') formation. In the words of Gregory Currie, to compose a fiction the writer must have a 'fiction-making intention': 'The author intends that we make-believe the text (or rather its constituent propositions) and he intends to get us to do this by means of our recognition of that very intention' (Currie 1990: 31). I discussed this view in Chapter 3 where I argued that it was vitiated by the consensus view having no account of what it is to 'make-believe' a proposition that links such propositions to fiction. In the next two chapters I shall add some detail to my alternative account.

I have claimed that a more illuminating approach is to divide the problem into two tasks: first that of providing an account of engaging with representations that is neutral between non-fiction and fiction, and second that of providing an account of the relations between the propositions in the representations and our pre-existing structures of belief. 'Engaging with' a representation includes, but is not necessarily exhausted by, understanding the representation. I will defend this approach in five stages. First, I shall provide some persuasive considerations for thinking of matters in this way. Second, I will support my approach with evidence from psychology. Third, I will consider an objection: that it is in the nature of beliefs that they cohere while it is not in the nature of make-beliefs that they cohere. Hence, the processing of beliefs is subject to different constraints to the processing of make-beliefs, and thus we cannot give an account of engaging with representations that is neutral between the non-fiction and fiction. Fourth—in the next chapter—I will provide some detail concerning the relations between the processing of representations and our pre-existing structures of belief. Finally, I will say a little (as that is all that need be said) about what it is for a representation to be fictional.

There are three good reasons for thinking our engaging with representations is neutral between non-fiction and fiction. The first reason is that this is the position the consensus view on the imagination is committed to anyway. As we have seen, the consensus view is that imagination is a matter of running mental states offline. Amongst the mental states we run offline will be beliefs; indeed, all that it needs for a mental state to be run offline is that we are not in a confrontation relation with its content. So, by the consensus view's own lights, the content of what we imagine is neutral between being non-fictional and being fictional.

The second good reason also follows from what has come before. In a representation relation we have two tasks, neither of which we have in a confrontation relation. The first task is to understand the representation. It is an important necessary condition of engaging with a verbal representation that we understand it in the basic sense; that is, we understand the words and the sentences in which it is written. Clearly, this task is neutral between non-fiction and fiction; we do not understand a literal sentence from a biography in a different manner to which we understand a literal sentence from a novel. In both cases all we need is (for readers of this book at least) a grasp of English. The second task, which applies to all but thin representations, is to make it vivid to ourselves. For thin representations this is not necessary; all I need to do to engage with my wife's note to cancel the order for milk is to understand the sentences contained therein. However, to use the standard metaphor, thick representations 'transport' us into other worlds. Richard Gerrig spells this out at length, providing examples from verbal representations and different forms of depictive representations (Gerrig 1993: 2-17). However, the essence of the point can be stated succinctly:

This metaphor [of being transported], in fact, goes a long way toward capturing one of the most prominent phenomenological aspects of the experience of narrative worlds. Readers become 'lost in a book'; moviegoers are surprised when the lights come back up; television viewers care desperately about the fates of soap opera characters; museum visitors are captivated by the stories encoded in daubs of paint. In each case, a narrative serves to transport an experiencer away from the here and now. (Gerrig 1993: 3)

Some mechanism is needed which will take as input (in verbal representations) the words on the page and as output being transported to another world. Being thus transported may well be a necessary condition for having the 'p-responses' (including emotional responses) described above. Intuitively, without making any heavy theoretical commitments, it is plausible to think of that mechanism as the imagination. Whatever the mechanism is, it will need to be neutral between a non-fictional input and a fictional input. Richard Holmes' biography of the Duke of Wellington needs to transport us to the field of Waterloo quite as much as Tolstoy's *War and Peace* needs to transport us to the battle of Austerlitz.[1]

The third reason for thinking of our attitude to the content of representations as being neutral between non-fictions and fictions is that it accommodates the fact that we do not need to know whether a representation is non-fictional or fictional in order to engage with it. The experience of reading de Quincey's 'The Revolt of the Tartars' is the same whether we believe it is non-fictional, believe it is fictional, or (as is most likely) we are ignorant of whether it is non-fictional or fictional (in fact, it is a highly fictionalized account of actual events). Our engaging with the representation is unaffected by this information, so our account of what it is to engage with a representation should make no use of this information.

Why, then, does the consensus view link imagination exclusively to engagement with fiction? The answer appears to be something like this. Understanding a representation involves our constructing a mental model of its content. In the case of the biography of the Duke of Wellington we are intended to believe the content of the mental model. In the case of a fiction we are not intended to believe it rather we are intended to make-believe it. However, as we have seen, fictions are a patchwork of propositions we are intended to believe and those we are not intended to believe. The consensus view then has the self-inflicted problem of sorting the former from the latter without excluding the former from being part of the content of fiction. A more plausible solution is to hold that, at the stage at which we are

---

[1] In this Gerrig agrees—'I intend *narrative* and *narrative world* to be neutral with respect to the issue of fictionality' (Gerrig 1993: 7).

building a mental model of the content of a representation in our heads, our attitudes to the individual propositions is not one of either belief or make-belief. In as much as we have an attitude to them at all, it is merely one of them being part of the content of whatever particular representation we are reading or remembering. We may have an attitude to the *representation* as to it being fictional and non-fictional (as we shall see) but that is a different matter.

If the claim that our engagement with representations is neutral between non-fiction and fiction, we would expect this fact to be reflected in psychology. The question concerns whether the mental models formed on the basis of engaging with representations integrate directly into existing knowledge structures or whether they are 'compartmentalized'. We can hypothesize two models. The 'structural model' holds that the information from the representation is compartmentalized: that is, a new 'node' is created in memory to store the information ('nodes' and 'connections' among them are metaphors used by cognitive psychologists to describe memory structures (Gerrig 1993: 213)). The 'context directed search model' holds that information from the representation is incorporated directly into existing memory structures. George Potts and his colleagues have run a number of experiments to test which model we use (Potts, St. John et al. 1989). In their experiments subjects read a representation—which they are told is non-fiction—concerning the near extinction of a New Zealand bird, the takahe. Potts and his colleagues worked on the assumption that 'the primary functional characteristic of compartmentalized information is that it is difficult to retrieve that information in a context that is different from the one in which it is learned' (Potts, St. John et al. 1989: 305). What Potts and colleagues did (putting matters crudely) was to ask about the content of the story in story contexts and in non-story contexts. If the structural model were correct, there would be little direct connection between the takahe and information about birds held in existing memory structures, and hence the time it took to retrieve information in story contexts would be less than the time it took to retrieve information in non-story contexts. If the context directed search model were correct, then there would be a direct connection between the takahe and what was already known about birds and this time difference would not be apparent.

The results of the tests supported the structural model: 'there were few direct associations between the new concepts and their real world

superordinates, suggesting that the compartmentalization of new information does involve some kind of structural separation between the old
and new information' (Potts, St. John et al. 1989: 332). This should not be
overstated: Potts and colleagues also found that information from what
readers believed were non-fictional representations were assimilated
more easily into existing memory structures than information from
what readers believed were fictional representations (this will be quali-
fied below). However, the result is remarkable; the mental model readers construct from a representation is 'held' at a new node, rather than
integrated directly into existing memory structures. This is true whether
the representation is non-fictional or fictional. At the very least this provides some support from psychology for the philosophical view that the
most perspicuous way to construe our engaging with representations is
to see the processing of representations as neutral as to whether they are
non-fiction or fiction.

Compartmentalization does not, of course, mean isolation. That
is, there is an interaction between the content of the narrative and the
reader's structures of belief. As we have seen, the nature of this interaction depends in part on whether the reader believes the narrative to be
non-fiction or fiction. In cases where the reader believes the narrative to
be fictional the interaction also depends on the nature of the information; that is, whether it is specific to the fiction or applies to the world
outside the fiction (Gerrig and Prentice 1991). We will return to this
point below.

The claim that we can give an account of understanding a representation that is neutral between non-fictional and fictional representations
might be thought to face an obvious counterexample. We have seen that
text comprehension depends on the reader establishing local coherence.
If local coherence breaks down, or knowledge is not easily available, or
if there is some strategy beyond reading for comprehension, the reader
will attempt to establish global coherence. Given that engaging with a representation of even marginal thickness seems to count as having 'some
strategy beyond reading for comprehension,' we can assume the readers
in whom we are interested engage with global as well as local coherence.
Hence, I shall assume the constructivist rather than the minimalist position. This is dialectically sound, as the difficulty of establishing that there
is no difference between processing non-fiction and processing fiction
will increase with the richness of the mental model.

Graesser and his colleagues give us the following sketch of local and global coherence:

The explicit statements in a text need to be connected conceptually if the text is to be regarded as coherent. Local coherence is achieved if the reader can connect the incoming statement to information in the previous sentence or WM [working memory]. Global coherence is achieved if the incoming statement can be connected to a text macrostructure or to information much earlier in the text that no longer resides in WM. Readers normally attempt to achieve coherence at both the local and global levels...Suppose, for example, that a character is described as a vegetarian early in the text and that much later the text states that the character ate a hamburger. The contradiction could only be detected if the reader were attempting to achieve global coherence. Reading times have been found to increase for such contradictory statements under conditions in which the statement *X is a vegetarian* has no local connections to *X ate a hamburger*. This increase in reading time would not occur if text comprehension was driven entirely by local connections. However, it is important to acknowledge that attempts at achieving global coherence will diminish and local coherence will dominate if the text is incoherent, if the reader is unmotivated, or if the reader has a low WM. Comprehension suffers substantially when neither local nor global coherence can be achieved...As a general underlying principle, readers attempt to achieve the most global level of understanding that can be achieved given the text composition, the reader's knowledge base, and the reading goals. (Graesser, Millis et al. 1997: 178)

The grounds for scepticism regarding the claim that non-fiction and fiction are processed in the same way are obvious: non-fiction and fiction differ in that what is incoherent in the former is not necessarily incoherent in the latter. Incoherence in non-fiction is a matter of it not being the case that a set of propositions could all be true at once. In some fictions (such as magic realism and science fiction) such a set would not necessarily be incoherent. Thus, the text processing in the case of non-fiction runs on different rules to the text processing in the case of fiction.

The broader problem of which this is part concerns the principles by which the reader 'constructs' the content of a representation. Representations (that is, verbal representations), whether they are non-fictions or fictions, contain a limited amount of explicit information. It is left to the reader to 'fill in the gaps'. A representation about a wolf may not make it explicit that the wolf is dangerous yet we can take it to be part of the content of the representation that the wolf is dangerous. It is worth noting that, as was discussed in the last chapter, the detail of the mental model that readers construct will vary not only from reader to reader, but also from occasion to occasion. If readers are being minimalist their mental model will be an ever-changing set of locally coherent propositions. Constructivism suggests a richer mental model, but the psychological reality of even these will fall far short of completeness. We can relate the reader's mental model to the content of the representation by thinking of the content as an idealization; something like the mental model that would be constructed by some idealized reader in idealized circumstances.[2] No matter how idealized, such a model will be indeterminate. The narrative about the wolf is unlikely to specify whether the number of hairs on the wolf is odd or even.

The case of non-fictional representations appears relatively straightforward. The explicit information is coherent if all the propositions in it could be true together. The background (or 'derived information') is whatever was true in the actual world where and when the events in the narrative occurred (and we can interpret 'world' to mean 'universe'). For some, this is counterintuitive. Consider the narrative of a wedding party in the Cotswolds. Is it really part of the content of that narrative that there is instability in the Middle East and that the Milky Way is vast? One reason for thinking it is is that the narrative could be supplemented in surprising ways. Someone could joke that the passage to the register being signed in the Cotswolds was as fraught with uncertainty as the passage to a treaty being signed in Jerusalem, or the best man could compare the size of the bridegroom's ego unfavourably with the size of the Milky Way. Such comments, which are eminently comprehensible, would make no sense if the uncertainty in the Middle East or the size of the Milky Way was not part of the wedding narrative.

The important point is that the above considerations cannot be used to ground a distinction between non-fictional and fictional representations as exactly the same considerations govern many fictional representations. The content of a fictional representation is given by what would have been true in the actual world were the events described in the fiction to have happened in the actual world. This is one of two different principles David Lewis offers us in his paper 'Truth in Fiction' (I shall not discuss the other):

A sentence of the form 'In the fiction f, φ' is non-vacuously true iff some world where f is told as known fact and φ is true differs less from our actual world, on

---

[2]   This is related to Walton's definition: 'A proposition is fictional, let's say, if it is to be imagined (in the relevant context) should the question arise, it being understood that often the question shouldn't arise' (Walton 1990: 40). However, it does not suffer from the problem that a representation can mandate that we imagine something, without that thing being part of its content. (This problem is discussed in an as yet unpublished paper by Walton.)

balance, than does any world where f is told as known fact and φ is not true. It is vacuously true iff there are no possible worlds where f is told as known fact. (Lewis 1978: 42)

The details need not matter for our purposes (although we will return to the question of why Lewis and others claim that we need to imagine, of our engagement with fiction, that it is an engagement with non-fiction). What I want to discuss here is what Kendall Walton later called 'the reality principle':

If $p_1, \ldots, p_n$ are the propositions whose fictionality a representation generates directly, another proposition, q, is fictional in it if, and only if, were it the case that $p_1, \ldots, p_n$, it would be the case that q. (Walton 1990: 145)

The claim is that we fit the actual world around the explicit information in the representation; the actual world provides the background and the basis for inference. Were Holmes to have lived in London in the late nineteenth century he would have lived in a city with a population of roughly five million, so it is part of the content of the stories that he lives in a city with a population of roughly five million. Furthermore, other facts that were true of London when the story was set are also part of the content. We might need to draw on the fact that London is a certain distance from Dover to understand why Holmes, in London, gives up trying to arrest the malefactors he knows to be in Dover in the process of boarding a ship.

Peter Lamarque and Stein Olsen disagree with the approach taken here. They argue that, in fictional contexts, there is reason to think referring terms have only their sense and not their reference. Furthermore, 'these reasons do not apply outside fiction'.

...the fictive stance generates something like a non-extensional context; only 'something like' because strictly this is just an analogy. The common tests for extensionality are (1) substitutivity of co-referential terms *salva veritate*, and (2) applicability of the rule of existential generalisation (the inference from 'a is F' to 'something is F'). Although extra-fictional names in fictive utterances do submit to existential generalisation they are subject to something analogous to failure of substitutivity *salva veritate*. As truth is not at issue, let us speak instead of *salva fictione*. In short, *story-identity is not preserved under some substitutions of co-referential singular terms* in fictive utterances. To take a trivial example, if the sentence 'Holmes returned to London' appears in a Conan Doyle story we have not preserved the story, or its content, if we substitute a sentence equivalent in truth-value and reference, such as 'Holmes returned to the Smoke' or even 'Holmes returned to the city where Mrs Thatcher lives.' (Lamarque and Olsen 1994: 80–1)

In a footnote, Lamarque and Olsen rightly point out that the fact that Mrs Thatcher lived in London many years after the Holmes stories were set does not make a difference. The example could simply be changed to 'Holmes returned to the city where Mrs Thatcher was later to live.' There are two separate points of disagreement here. The first is that singular terms contribute differently to the content of fictional narratives than they do to the content of non-fictional narratives. The second is that, in a fictional narrative, the meaning of singular terms is a matter of their sense rather than their reference. As I hold that what is true of singular terms in fictional narratives is also true of them in non-fictional narratives, I will need to consider this latter point for all narratives.

That Lamarque and Olsen are wrong on the first point is easily shown. Whatever the intuitions harnessed in the Sherlock Holmes example are harnessed equally in a non-fictional narrative. The sentence 'When Wellington rode to his official residence, No 10 Downing Street, on Copenhagen, the charger he had ridden at Waterloo, he was making a political point' occurs in Richard Holmes eminently non-fictional biography of Wellington (Holmes 1996: 271). Whatever qualms we feel in the Holmes case, we would surely also feel if we substituted the sentence 'When Wellington rode to his official residence, the house later to be occupied by Mrs Thatcher, on Copenhagen, the charger he had ridden at Waterloo, he was making a political point.' Mention of Mrs Thatcher is no more appropriate in a non-fictional biography of Wellington than it is in the fictional Holmes stories.

Lamarque and Olsen show that substituting co-referring singular terms in a narrative can change the sense of the narrative. They rightly conclude that such singular terms 'cannot be purely denotative' (Lamarque and Olsen 1994: 81). However, it is surely unsurprising that substituting one singular term for a co-referring singular term (particularly where the latter is fairly outlandish) will change the meaning of the sentence in which that singular term is embedded; that is simply a consequence of meaning being composed of both sense and reference (or pragmatics as well as semantics). To license their stronger conclusion—'a sense for the names in fiction... captures *all and only* the relevant aspects of the objects named' (Lamarque and Olsen 1994: 82—the italics are mine)—they would need to show that a name having any denotative function is *incompatible* with its contribution to a fictional narrative. To do this they would need to show more than that, in a fictional narrative set in the nineteenth century, it would (usually)[3] be wholly inappropriate to refer to it as the future home of Mrs Thatcher. They would need to show that, in a fictional narrative set in the nineteenth century, London is not the future home of Mrs Thatcher. However, this is a stronger conclusion than their arguments license. That the future abode of Mrs Thatcher is not (usually) brought up in a fictional narrative (or indeed any narrative) set in the nineteenth century is accounted for by the fact that doing so would violate the principles of conversational implicature and, in doing so, would make it impossibly difficult for the listener to construct the kind of mental model that would enable him or her to engage with the narrative. Everything is already accounted for without the need to rule out singular terms keeping their denotative function.

Having considered Lamarque and Olsen's objection, let us return to the reality principle and focus on the claim that it does not govern what counts as incoherence in the text processing of fiction. As stated above, that claim is too crude. The reality principle *does* underpin text processing for many fictions: namely, all fictions in which the background is, indeed, the actual world. Furthermore, as Kendall Walton has pointed out, if we take into account the extended engagement we might have with fiction (namely, wondering about the motivations of the characters, doing a bit of background research into the historical situations in which they find themselves) that also fits neatly into the reality principle.

The process of discovering what is fictional in the work makes it fictional of him in the game that he discovers what is true. [The Reality Principle] is especially conducive to such participation, since investigations of fictional worlds in accordance with it mirror investigations of the real world. (Walton 1990: 159)

Clearly the division is not between non-fiction and fiction, but between representations which take the actual world as background and representations which do not take the actual world as background.

Accepting all the forgoing, it nonetheless remains to be shown that there is a single principle underlying the search for coherence of all representations, whether non-fictional or fictional. Let me first describe an idealized situation. Readers begin engaging with a representation with no

---

[3] The qualifier is necessary because it is possible for there to be a narrative (non-fictional or fictional) set in the nineteenth century that uses the fact of London being the future abode of Mrs Thatcher.

presuppositions as to what would count as coherent in that representation. As they read they form an impression as to what will and will not
count as incoherent. Against the background of that impression, they
evaluate possible candidates for incoherence as being either really incoherent (and thus look for possible explanations) or simply more information as to what will and will not count as incoherent in that representation.
They read on, undertaking a form of reflective equilibrium, questioning
whether some of the states of affairs described in the representation are
coherent while accepting others.

My claim is that this underlies our engagement with all representations. Generally, however, we are able to short-circuit the process, which
is just as well as it would be remarkably inefficient to start from scratch
with each representation we encounter. We short-circuit it by knowing the
kind of representation it is with which we are engaged. With non-fiction
it is easy; we can assume from the outset that the reality principle holds.
This is also the case with much fiction—it will be apparent from what we
have heard about the book, from what we know of the author's oeuvre, or
from what we read on the back, that the reality principle holds. However,
with other genres such as magic realism and science fiction we do not
assume the reality principle holds. In such cases we need to feel our way
forward: deaths are not final if there is some possibility (which there is not,
according to the reality principle) of coming back to life and we need to
read on to find out if, in this representation, coming back to life is allowed.
There may even be non-fictional genres that do not rely on the reality
principle. A very precise research scientist might have a genre of 'idealized
reports of experiments' in which such things as air resistance and other
forms of friction are ignored. These may well, to his or her practiced eye,
come out as strictly incoherent on the reality principle, and thus he or she
will read them with a different benchmark for incoherence in mind.

The fact that we feel our way forward can be used to great aesthetic effect
by clever authors. Mikhail Bulgakov's *The Master and Margarita* is, stylis-
tically, in the tradition of Russian realist fiction except that it is punctuated
by episodes that are weirdly incoherent according to the reality principle.
The reader gradually realizes that the Devil has in fact come to Moscow
and that there is a sharp-shooting cat travelling on public transport. The
reader's initial struggle to reconcile events with the reality principle neatly
mirrors the Soviet apparatchik's struggle, within the novel, to reconcile
events with the official doctrine of atheistic materialism. There is much

more to be said about both coherence and about genre. I shall return to
the former topic when I discuss impossible fictions in Chapter 9. My purpose here has been to blunt the force of an argument against my view that
our understanding of representations is neutral between non-fiction and
fiction by arguing for two conclusions. First, the division between representations that do and representations that do not conform to the reality
principle does not correspond to the distinction between non-fiction and
fiction. Second, there is a principle for working out what principles under-
lie coherence and generate content which is true for all representations.

It might be thought that the consensus view could concede this point,
as there remains an underlying difference in the way we process representations that is systematically different between non-fictions and fictions. To see this, we need to look again at something we encountered in
Chapter 2: what Walton calls 'principles of generation'. These are the general principles by which we move from the claims made in the text to the
content of our mental model of the representation. Consider the following
example from Walton:

> Recall the suicide of Mrs. Verloc on her voyage to the Continent in Conrad's *Secret
> Agent*. The newspaper headline, 'Suicide of a Lady Passenger from a cross-Channel
> Boat,' informs the reader of her death. But how can we jump so irresponsibly to
> the conclusion that she was the victim? We have some additional circumstantial
> evidence, to be sure. We know that Mrs. Verloc was distraught after having killed
> her husband, and was afraid of the gallows. Earlier she had contemplated drown-
> ing herself in the Thames. Ossipon had abandoned her on the train and stolen her
> money. But little if any of this additional evidence is needed to establish the fact
> that fictionally it was Mrs. Verloc who jumped from the ferry. And even this evi-
> dence would, in a real case, stand in need of confirmation; there could easily have
> been another suicidal passenger crossing the Channel the same night. It is doubt-
> ful at best that, were a newspaper to carry that headline in those circumstances, it
> would have been Mrs. Verloc who had jumped (or even that it would have been
> more likely than not that it was she) ... Yet there is no doubt whatever that, fiction-
> ally, the suicide was hers. (Walton 1990: 162)

The claim here is that there are certain inferences we can make in fiction (from the scanty evidence of the newspaper headline to the death of
Mrs Verloc) that we would not be justified in making in the actual world.
I have no dispute with that claim, however it is nothing to do with fiction. We make the same sorts of inferences in non-fiction that we would
not be justified in making in the real world. The inference would not be
one we would be justified in making in a confrontation relation (which,

of course, happens in the actual world) however that is not the point at issue. The relevant contrast is not that between inferences we would make in fictions against those we would make in confrontation relations, but between inferences we would make in fictions against those we would make in non-fictions. That is, are the habits of inference we exhibit when we engage with fiction systematically different from those we exhibit when we engage with non-fiction? The example does nothing to show that there is such a difference. That is, the technique of mentioning a detail and leaving the reader to make the inference is a technique of narrative as such rather than fictional narratives in particular. It is easy to find similar examples in non-fictional narratives. Consider the ending of Frederic Morton's *A Nervous Splendour*:

On Saturday 20th April, the day before Easter, at 4 p.m., Mozart's 'Te Deum' was sung in the Court Chapel a few yards from Rudolf's old apartment. Professor Anton Bruckner drew great chords and holy harmonies from the organ to celebrate the Resurrection. While the master's august music rose among the vaultings, a different sound was heard in Bruckner's native Upper Austria at Braunau. It was the thin cry of a baby born that afternoon. The parents were Alois and Klara Hitler. They named their little one Adolf. (Morton 2006: 211)

In the actual world, we simply have a number of simultaneous events. The glorious music of Mozart in the Chapel and the bawling of Mr and Mrs Hitler's baby some way off in the mountains. However, by placing the two events side by side in the narrative, Morton makes it true in the narrative that it will be the latter that brings the world of the former to a final termination. All narratives, whether fiction or non-fiction, generate content through juxtaposition, the picking out of details, the use of ad hoc symbolism, and so on. Hence, the example of Mrs Verloc does not support the claim that processing fictional representations runs on different principles to processing non-fictional representations; it supports the rival claim— the claim for which I have been arguing—that the fundamental distinction is between a representation (in which they are, or could be, justified) and a confrontation (in which these inferences would not be justified).

Walton has rightly claimed that principles of generation have grown up in an unsystematic and ad hoc manner: 'The machinery of generation is devised of rubber bands and paper clips and powered by everything from unicorns in traces to baking soda mixed with vinegar' (Walton 1990: 183). My point is only that these principles are not characteristic of fiction but characteristic of representations (whether fictions or non-fictions). Walton points out that any nearly naked man pierced by arrows in medieval or Renaissance Christian art will be Saint Sebastian (Walton 1990: 163). This will be the case whether the narrative is (taken to be) non-fiction or fiction; the principle of generation works in either case. It is true that there are certain principles of generation that have grown up within the institution of fiction—even fiction which obeys the reality principle—which cannot be found in non-fictional narratives. To take an example from Panofsky cited by Walton, it might be that even in a realist fiction a chequered tablecloth means 'a poor but honest milieu' (Walton 1990: 163). Once again, that is nothing special about fiction. There are similar conventions in non-fiction which enables, for example, editors of news reports to use an opening in which a family is taking tea around the dining-room table to establish at least the presumption that the family is 'normal.'

So far I have given philosophical arguments for thinking of our engaging with narratives as neutral between non-fiction and fiction, supported this with some evidence from psychology, and considered an apparent problem for the claim. In the next chapter, I will go on to add some details about the relation between our engagement with the narrative and our pre-existing structures of belief.

7

Narrative and Belief

In the last chapter I argued for a 'two stage' model of engaging with representations. The first stage is neutral between non-fictional and fictional representations: we build a mental model of the representation that is compartmentalized but not isolated from our pre-existing structures of belief. In this chapter I will say more about the second stage: the relation between this engagement and our structures of belief.[1] I am concerned, in this discussion, about beliefs we form on engaging with narratives that are not about those narratives as narratives. That is, I will put aside the unproblematic case of beliefs such as (for example) our forming the belief, on opening *Moby Dick*, that the first sentence of *Moby Dick* is 'Call me Ishmael.'

I shall begin with non-fictional narratives. I shall assume that a Gricean model of explanation applies: that the author intends us to believe the propositions that form the content of the narrative on the grounds of our recognition of that intention (plus whatever epicycles that need to be gone through to make this account defensible (Blackburn 1984: 110-140)). Of course, as we have seen, it might not be straightforward to ascertain the content; one might need to interpret metaphors or other literary tropes. However, such interpretation having been done, we are mandated to believe the propositions that form the narrative's content. This does not, of course, entail that we should believe them. The mandate may be overridden, primarily by the belief that the effusions of the author do not track the truth. However, in the ideal situation, there is nothing to prevent the propositions that form the content of our mental model from being integrated into our pre-existing structures of belief.

---

[1] Some of the key ideas in this chapter are anticipated in Friend (2006). Friend's subsequent modification of her view (2014) is also contains relevant information.

Despite the contrast I drew in the last chapter between my account and that of Peter Lamarque and Stein Olson, there are some similarities between our two accounts on which I would like to draw. They describe themselves as having a 'no truth theory of literature' (Lamarque and Olsen 1994: 1). The label can be misleading. It is not that they think that literature cannot give us knowledge. Rather, their concern is to discover 'what role such knowledge plays in literary appreciation' (Lamarque and Olsen 1994: 13). That is, they acknowledge that there are propositions that are part of the content of fictions that we would be right to come to believe. What they stress is that such propositions have a dual function: first, the role they play (in my terms) in the mental model the reader builds of the content and, second, the role they play as beliefs. Here is what they say about propositions that are part of the content of a fiction that are candidates for belief:

Perhaps the best solution to this perennial problem is, at least from the point of view of fiction (if not literature), to invoke the category of factual content subject to the fictive stance, that is, content of a factual nature presented in the fictive mode and integrated into a wider fictional content. Being fact-oriented the content is amenable to truth assessment and might serve to impart belief, and be intended to do so; being subject to the fictive stance it occupies a distinctive role in reflection on fictional content and in the characterization of a fictional world. (Lamarque and Olsen 1994: 66–7)

I take this to be an accurate description of the situation, provided one substitutes the word 'narrative' for 'fiction' (and its derivatives), where 'narrative' covers non-fictions and fictions. However, Lamarque and Olsen's view that fiction is an important and distinctive category raises a question for them, their answer to which seems to me to weaken their position. The question is whether the truth or falsity of the factual content makes a difference to the role that content has when taken as part of the fiction. Lamarque and Olsen argue that, being part of a fiction, that proposition is subject to the fictive stance and the fictive stance involves imagining the proposition, and further, that 'truth and falsity are indifferent to what is possible to imagine' (Lamarque and Olsen 1994: 43, 60). This drives them to the conclusion that the role a proposition plays as part of a fictional narrative is independent of its truth value (Lamarque and Olsen 1994: 321–38). That is, they are committed to the view that when we are engaged with a fictional narrative as a fictional narrative, our engagement is radically compartmentalized. The truth or otherwise of the factual content makes no difference to either our understanding of the narrative or to the value we ascribe to it. That seems a conclusion best avoided. It is counterintuitive to think that, as we read a fiction as a fiction, with all the asides from the author or general claims about the nature of the world, it makes no difference at all whether or not those claims are true. The approach I favour holds that we engage with a narrative as a narrative: there is no 'fictive stance'. Hence, I am not committed to the content being radically compartmentalized from our beliefs. Indeed, I have argued that there is traffic between the content of the fiction and our structures of belief. Thus, the approach has more flexibility than Lamarque and Olsen's approach; in particular, it is open to the possibility that false factual claims do affect our understanding of, and our evaluation of, fictional narratives.

As we have seen, the consensus view holds that a proposition is fictional if there is a mandate to imagine it. A popular candidate for the source of this mandate is that the author has a Gricean intention that the reader imagine the proposition: the author intends the reader to make-believe the propositions that form the content of the narrative on the grounds of his or her recognition of that intention (as we have seen, Walton is an exception to this (Walton 1990: 52–3)). Whether or not the mechanism we favour for setting up the mandate is Gricean, the view has a problem. There are many propositions that are part of the content of fictional works that the reader is mandated to believe rather than make-believe.

I doubt whether there is any systematic way of distinguishing, within the content of a fiction, those propositions a reader ought to believe and those a reader ought to engage with but not believe. Peter Lamarque makes some helpful initial distinctions:

One is between *explicit* propositional content, in the form of indicative sentences within works, and *derived* propositional content, the result of a reader's reconstruction of explicit content through inference and 'filling in'. Another distinction is between subject-level content and thematic-level content. The distinctions cut across each other. Subject-level content can be both explicit and derived, as can thematic-level content. By subject-level content is meant the characters, events, episodes, experiences, presented in a work, from an emotional predicament in a short lyric to a complex narrative in a novel. Such content is often, but not necessarily, fictional, in the sense of being made up. Derived subject content is that supplementary content filled in, imaginatively or inferentially, by a reader. Thematic-level content, in contrast, is rarely fictional and involves generalizations, sometimes explicitly given, sometimes derived by readers, on the work's subject. (Lamarque 2010: 373)

As Lamarque says, although authors of fictions usually make up explicit subject level content, material concerning 'characters, events, episodes, experiences' can also be true. Authors can use this opportunity to give readers new beliefs. For example, Herman Melville communicates, through *Moby Dick*, facts about nineteenth century whaling practices and Graham Swift communicates, through *Waterland*, facts about the history of the fen landscape.[2] The communication can sometimes be quite subtle. When, in *Tender is the Night*, Fitzgerald has the usually unreliable Nicole Diver say 'Most people think everybody feels about them much more violently than they actually do' the reader takes it not only to be true in the fiction that Nicole says this, but takes what she says to be true *simpliciter* (Scott Fitzgerald 2005: 63). According to Lamarque explicit thematic level content is usually true, although it can be made up. The generalizations on the nature of love readers derive from *Tender is the Night* are true, and intended by Fitzgerald to be believed.

Truths can be communicated within the content of fiction by ways other than subject level content and thematic level content. The author can take the unusual step of directly addressing the reader in his or her own voice. Kathleen Stock gives a nice example from *Vanity Fair*:

When one man has been under very remarkable obligations to another, with whom he subsequently quarrels, a common sense of decency, as it were, makes of the former a much severer enemy than a mere stranger would be. To account for your own hard-heartedness and ingratitude in such a case, you are bound to prove the other party's crime.[3] (Stock 2011: 148)

This passage looks to be a standard instance of attempted Gricean communication.

The extent to which derived content is true will vary to the extent to which the reality principle applies. Even where the reality principle does apply, some of the propositions that make up the derived content will not be candidates for belief; that is, some of the derived content will be fictional implications of fictional explicit content. However, much of the derived content will be true. For example, facts about the history,

---

[2] In an epigram to the book, Swift cites a definition of 'Historia': '1. inquiry, investigation, learning. 2. a) a narrative of past events, history. b) any kind of narrative: account, tale, story.' (*Waterland*, 1984, London: Picador).

[3] The reference Stock provides is *Vanity Fair*, 2003, New York: Spark Educational Publishing, pg. 176.

geography, and politics of early nineteenth-century Europe will be part of the derived content of *War and Peace*. Readers will need to bring this content from their structures of belief into their mental models of the content of the narrative. It is not the case that all such derived content need already be known; we can learn facts about the world from derived content that is implied by explicit content.

Psychology also has a contribution to make to the distinction we are drawing here between propositions that are true only in fiction and propositions that are both true in fiction and true *simpliciter*. Prentice and Gerrig constructed a number of representations the content of which they sorted into two broad types.

One type consisted of 'context details'—features of the story setting that were specific to that particular fictional world. For example, our stories contained information about the identity of the president and vice-president of the United States, the national speed limit, and the city and time of year in which the story was taking place. A second type of information consisted of 'context free assertions'—general statements that were not conditioned upon particular features of the fictional world. For example, our stories included arguments about the beneficial versus detrimental health consequences of penicillin and aerobic exercise, the contagiousness of mental illness, and the effects of legacy status on college admissions. (Prentice and Gerrig 1999: 536).

The distinction Prentice and Gerrig are attempting to mark (which is not altogether clear from this description) is information that is true in the fiction in which there is no presumption that it is true *simpliciter* and information that is true in the fiction in which there is a presumption that it is true *simpliciter*. I shall return to this shortly.

The fact that the propositions that make up the content of a fiction are a mixture of those that are, and those that are not, also true *simpliciter* raises an epistemological problem for the reader. For any particular proposition, how does a reader know whether to believe it? The problem does not arise for those propositions a reader already believes (whether these are derived or explicit propositions). As I said above, I do not think there is any systematic way in which we can distinguish those propositions that are candidates for belief from those propositions that are not candidates for belief. As Lamarque and Olsen point out, 'If a story-teller uses the description 'the capital of England' then there is a presumption that he intends to refer to London but if he uses the phrase 'the head of the Civil Service' it cannot be presumed that he is referring to whoever happens to be the head of the Civil Service at the time of writing' (Lamarque and Olsen 1994: 109). Readers are guided by such pointers as convention, contextual clues, and estimates of probability. Of course, like the comment Fitzgerald puts in the mouth of Nicole Diver, a proposition might simply strike one as true (and strike one as something Fitzgerald intended us to believe). A cautious scepticism is appropriate: it would be a rather naïve reader who accepted each 'context free assertion' as something to be believed. He or she would, arguably, be right in the case of the opening sentence of *Anna Karenina* ('Happy families are all alike; every unhappy family is unhappy in its own way') but wrong in the case of the opening sentence of *Pride and Prejudice* ('It is a truth universally acknowledged, that a single man in possession of a good fortune, must be in want of a wife.').

What underlies this cautious scepticism is that there is no presumption that propositions asserted within a fiction are true *simpliciter*. This is the central claim of the consensus view: narratives come in two types—those we are mandated to believe and those to which we are mandated to take some other attitude. Does my advocating cautious scepticism diminish the distance between my approach and that of the consensus view? There is some truth in this—that is, some truth in the irenic solution that I have simply found a different way of stating essentially the same problem. However, we need to remind ourselves of the crucial difference that stands between us and this irenic solution. The consensus view can only be stated by contrasting propositions we are mandated to believe with those to which we are mandated to take some other attitude. The consensus view has not succeeded in spelling out the nature of this attitude. As we have seen, their candidate ('make-believe' or 'imagining that') is hopeless as—by the view's own lights—that is the attitude we take to the content of representations generally rather than the content of fictions. My view suffers from no such defect. We represent (some part of) the content of a narrative with which we engage in a mental model. The narrative could be either non-fiction or fiction. Some of these propositions we also believe, some we do not also believe. That is it; there is no need, on this account, for us to wander into the swamp consequent on postulating a mental state particularly linked to fiction.

There are many reasons why a proposition that is part of a narrative with which we are engaged will not become a belief. It might be that we recognize that there is an intention that we form a belief but there are other reasons why we fail to form a belief; we might, for example, believe the intender to be unreliable. The truth in the irenic solution is that believing a narrative to be fictional is one of the reasons we have for failing to believe the propositions that form its content. However, the crucial difference remains: engaging with a narrative is a different issue from sorting out which propositions in that narrative to believe. Furthermore, as the consensus view has come to realize, there is no simple relation between a narrative being fictional and our not believing the propositions in that narrative. If a proposition in a fictional narrative does not become a belief, the proposition's role in our cognitive economy is only that of a proposition that forms part of the content of a narrative. It has this role in common with the other propositions that are part of the mental model we form on engaging with a narrative, whether non-fictional or fictional. If a proposition in a fictional narrative does become a belief, it has a role as a proposition that forms part of a narrative and it becomes a belief. This too, it has in common with other propositions that are part of the mental model we form on engaging with a narrative, whether non-fictional or fictional, that become beliefs.

The same point can be made if approached from a different direction. It is characteristic of narratives that engaging with them will be entertaining or, at least, interesting. In standard circumstances anyone who takes the trouble to construct a narrative will want it to have this function.[4] Narratives can have additional functions, of course, including (as we have seen) imparting beliefs. We recognize that some parts of some narratives are not intended to impart beliefs; their role is exhausted by their place in the mental model. This will be particularly true of those narratives we call 'fictional narratives'. A reader can, of course, ignore or downplay an author's intention that he or she forms beliefs on the basis of a narrative. Indeed, many readers of biographies surely do exactly this; a reader with no particular interest in (for example) eighteenth century Whig politics may nonetheless be highly entertained by being transported into that world through reading Amanda Foreman's biography, *The Duchess of Devonshire*. I have not been able to find any empirical research on the matter, but my prediction would be that the 'standard' consumer of biographies does not retain much of the content in the way of belief. They read

---

[4] As Peter Goldie stresses: 'thinking through a narrative, and narrating a narrative publicly, are kinds of *action*, done for reasons' (Goldie 2012: 150). Prominent amongst such reasons will be the desire to be entertaining or, at least, interesting.

the biography for the same reason as they read a novel; to be transported to a world, to be engrossed in a tale. It is surely no accident that, of the four reviews quoted on the back of the paperback issue of Foreman's biography, three praise it as being 'fascinating' and 'readable' while only one refers to its being 'extensively researched' (Foreman 1999).

Work in psychology brings out the sheer complexity of the relation between the content of fictional narratives and our pre-existing structures of belief. This research assumes some version of the compartmentalization model argued for by Potts and his colleagues. The question is the extent to which this compartmentalized content of a fictional narrative gets integrated into pre-existing structures of belief. Far from discovering that there is no such integration, the psychological evidence goes far in the other direction. There is a wealth of evidence to support the view that in comprehending a sentence we also accept the proposition it expresses (that is, we believe it) after which we go through a second stage of either certifying or 'unaccepting' that proposition (Gilbert 1991). In addition, engaging with a narrative known to be fiction can make one more or less inclined to affirm or deny claims about the actual world related to the content of that fiction (Gerrig 1993: 196–241; see also Marsh, Meade et al. 2003). Unsurprisingly, Potts and his colleagues found that there was greater integration when subjects believed they were engaging with non-fictional narratives: 'higher degrees of incorporation are achieved when subjects believe they are learning real information' (Potts, St. John et al. 1989: 331). Prentice and Gerrig conducted similar experiments, which largely duplicated these results. Readers created a new node to encode the story information, and context details were weakly linked to pre-existing structures while context-free details were strongly linked to pre-existing structures (Prentice and Gerrig 1999: 538). There were some rather unexpected results too. Readers who believed that they were reading fiction were more credulous as to its weak and unsupported context-free details. Prentice and Gerrig explain this by the fact that the subjects were processing what they believed was fiction less systematically and were subsequently less critically interrogative of the content.

Belief in fiction is determined not by a critical analysis of the strength of its arguments, but instead by the absence of motivation or ability to perform such an analysis. As a result, the persuasiveness of fiction depends less on its substance and more on rhetorical features of the narrative context and the expectations readers bring to it. (Prentice and Gerrig 1999: 542)

This discussion of the integration of some of the content of representations with pre-existing structures of belief should not draw our attention away from the main point. I have argued that authors create narratives, and readers engage with narratives, with certain purposes in mind. These might not be the same purposes: a narrative written for the purposes of communicating beliefs might be read for purposes of entertainment. Readers construct relatively sparse mental models of these narratives. This process can transport the reader to the world of the narrative and thus entertain him or her. There is also an interaction between this compartmentalized content and the reader's beliefs: the reader can supplement the content of the narrative from their beliefs, and their beliefs from the content of the narrative. Knowing that a narrative is fictional affects this correspondence; in short, the reader cannot presume the context details of the narrative are true.

I have focused on propositions in a narrative that a reader might already believe or might come to believe. However, there are other ways in which a narrative might inculcate new beliefs. In a thought-provoking paper Eileen John has argued that some fictions call upon us to consider how concepts apply in a particular case (in this way, they are somewhat akin to philosophical thought experiments). Reflecting on the fit between our intuitive use of a concept and its application within the fictional scenario can cause us to change our beliefs about that concept—even if we find such a change of beliefs hard to articulate (John 1998; see also Carroll 2000). Furthermore, we might come to believe the 'moral' of the narrative. A narrative, even a fictional narrative, can, like almost anything else, be a vehicle for a proposition (Walton 1990: 78; Lamarque and Olsen 1994: 64). *Sense and Sensibility* expresses the proposition that sense is a better approach to life than sensibility; Orwell's *1984* expresses the proposition that politics should not become detached from humanity.[5] Reading these narratives can convince us of the truth of these propositions.

I shall end this chapter by considering what some take to be the central problem in this area: that of providing a definition of 'fictional work'. The theme of this chapter has been that the relation between a narrative and our structures of belief is complicated. This is a problem for those who—unlike me—attempt to define 'fictional work' as one made up of

---

[5] Needless to say (I hope) these are not supposed to be reductive accounts of either the sense or point of the novels.

propositions we are intended to imagine rather than believe. However, my view seems to face an even greater problem. I have conceded that believing a narrative to be fictional makes a difference to a reader's attitude to the truth of the propositions that make up its content. What does a reader believe about a narrative if he or she believes that it is fictional?

The account I have given so far points to a way of answering that question. I have argued that one purpose, perhaps the main purpose, of engaging with narratives is entertainment. As this is the case, we are not constrained by truth in constructing our narratives (a made-up narrative gives more scope to bring in entertaining features than does one that is not made up). Thus, there is a tradition of constructing narratives that is not constrained by fidelity to what actually happened. Such narratives, as we have seen, will frequently be set in actual places, draw on actual events, and contain information new to the reader that it is intended the reader believe. We call narratives in this tradition 'fictional narratives'.

There is much work done by those who hold the consensus view on which I can draw (see, for example, (Currie 1990: 30–49; Carroll 1997; Davies 2007: 43–8; Stock 2011; an alternative view, closer to the one propounded here, can be found in Friend 2012)). David Davies succinctly expresses the point I am making:

> To read a narrative as non-fiction is to assume that the selection and temporal ordering of all the events making up the narrative was constrained by a desire, on the narrator's part, to be faithful to the manner in which actual events transpired. We assume that the author has included only events she believes to have occurred, narrated as occurring in the order in which she believes them to have occurred. We may term this the 'fidelity constraint'. To read a narrative as fiction, on the other hand, is to assume that the choices made in generating the narrative were not governed in the first instance by this constraint, but by some more general purpose in story-telling. (Davies 2007: 46)

To say that a particular narrative lies in a tradition in which authors are not bound by the fidelity constraint will not enable the reader to judge, of any particular proposition in the narrative, whether or not to believe it. As I said above, knowing that a narrative lies in this tradition should encourage readers to exercise a cautious scepticism. My account has the advantage over the consensus view on this point. The consensus view defines a fictional proposition as something a reader is mandated to imagine, where imagination is contrasted with belief. It then has the problem of moving from the definition of fictional proposition to the definition of fictional works, as such works contain many propositions we are mandated to believe (indeed, Kendall Walton has pointed out that there is nothing incoherent about a fiction consisting only of true sentences (Walton 1990: 79)). My view does not need a definition of fictional proposition: it needs only an understanding of what it is for a proposition to be part of the content of a narrative, and an account of the relation between engaging with a proposition and forming beliefs. On the latter score, knowing that the author did not obey the fidelity constraint, readers are left to fend for themselves.

Kendall Walton has pointed out that our concept of fiction is a 'rough everyday classification' (Walton 1990: 72). There are some books which are difficult to classify either as fictional or as non-fictional. Is Berkeley's *Three Dialogues of Hylas and Philonous* a fiction? It is not true that the audience is intended to believe that Hylas and Philonous utter what it is claimed that they utter, but the content of what they utter is intended to be weighed for truth. David Davies gives us examples of Seamus Deane's *Reading in the Dark* which won the Guardian Fiction Prize in 1996 despite being commissioned as an autobiography and despite the story in the book corresponding 'in all significant details to Deane's own childhood'. On the other side, in Blake Morrison's *When Did You Last See Your Father?* officially described as a memoir, 'Morrison changed not only the name of one of the protagonists but also the order in which some of the narrated events occur' (Davies 2007: 32). Stacie Friend's examples include Edmund Morris' *Dutch: A Memoir of Ronald Reagan* in which 'Morris (in)famously inserted himself in the story as a fictional narrator so that he could be on hand to witness many of the events in Reagan's life' and John Berndt's *Midnight in the Garden of Good and Evil*, classified as non-fiction, in which 'Berndt made up a scene and changed the chronology of some events in order to be present when a murder is committed' (Friend 2008: 150). There is the well-established genre of the 'new journalism', again classified as non-fiction, but which contained detailed descriptions of events that are 're-imagined' by the writer. Alexandra Fuller's memoir of growing up in Rhodesia, *Don't Let's Go to the Dogs Tonight* (winner of a prize for non-fiction), has all the hallmarks of a novel; it is written in the present continuous, with many re-imagined scenes, much free indirect speech, and a great deal of re-imagined dialogue. By contrast, Sybille Bedford's *Jigsaw*, also a memoir with all the hallmarks of a novel, is classified as fiction.[6]

---

[6] It is interesting to compare the account of Roy Campbell's visit to Aldous Huxley in *Jigsaw* with the account of the same event in Bedford's biography of Huxley (Bedford 1989: 253–255; Bedford 1993: 232–234).

It is also worth noting that the notion of the fictional itself is subject to change, as Stacie Friend has argued:

Despite frequently insisting that history must be restricted to the truth, Roman historians took this requirement to be compatible with the standard convention of making up speeches and battle descriptions. Tacitus's *Annals* and *Histories* are replete with vivid battles and strikingly eloquent speeches, the contents of which readers are not supposed to believe. In addition, Tacitus tells us what historical figures were thinking, including their dreams ... It was only in the late sixteenth century that historians began to eschew the presentation of inner thoughts, invented speeches or battles and the depiction of legendary heroes and fabulous events that had no basis in evidence. We could say that historical writing prior to the seventeenth and eighteenth century counts as fiction rather than non fiction. But surely it is more plausible to say that the conventions for writing non-fiction history have changed over time. (Friend 2012: 185)

Given the indeterminacy both in whether a particular narrative is fictional and in the divide between the fictional and the non-fictional, an approach that reflects this indeterminacy is to be preferred over one that does not (although Friend herself thinks we cannot do without the classification of narratives into the fictional and the non-fictional). Furthermore, the epicycles which the consensus view needs to add to achieve a definition of fictional work is surely a sign that something has gone wrong in the fundamentals of the account.

8

The (so-called) 'Paradox of Fiction'

Those who think our problems are peculiar to fiction, rather than to narratives more generally, might point out that it is impossible on the view I favour to explain how a certain familiar problem arises. I mean, of course, the much-discussed problem known as 'the paradox of fiction'. As an aside, I would claim that, if true, this is an advantage for the account. There has always been an air of artificiality about the problem (I except Walton's work from this charge) which suggests that, whatever the problem is, it has not been bought into sharp focus. I have not been able to discover where the phrase 'the paradox of fiction' came from. Colin Radford uses the term 'paradox' in well-known papers he wrote on the topic but never to name whatever he took to be the problem—which, as we shall see, is far from clear (Radford 1975; Radford 1977). It is an unfortunate misnomer, as the problem is neither a paradox nor is to do with fiction.

The way to understand the prolific confusion that characterizes this discussion is to approach the topic historically. There are intimations of a problem with psychological attitudes to fictional characters in Plato's *Ion*, St. Augustine's *Confessions*, and (famously) in Hamlet's speech to the player king, although, again, there is no clear idea of what the problem might be.[1] The modern debate seems to have begun with Colin Radford's paper, 'How Can We be Moved by the Fate of Anna Karenina?' Radford begins his paper with an example:

Suppose you read an account of the terrible sufferings of a group of people. If you are at all humane, you are unlikely to be unmoved by what you read. The account is likely to awaken or reawaken feelings of anger, horror, dismay or outrage, and, if you are tender-hearted, you may well be moved to tears. You may well even grieve.

---

[1] The references are *Confessions* 3.2; *Ion* 535 b-e; and *Hamlet*, II ii 533–46. I am grateful to Tim Chappell for the first two references.

But now suppose you discover the account is false. If the account had caused you to grieve, you could not continue to grieve. If as the account sank in, you were told and believed that it was false, this would make tears impossible unless they were tears of rage. If you learned later that the account was false, you would feel that in being moved to tears you had been fooled, duped. (Radford 1975: 240–1)

From this, Radford concludes that 'I can only be moved by someone's plight if I believe that something terrible has happened to him ... When we say that the thought ... moves us to tears or grieves us, it is thinking of or contemplating suffering which we believe to be actual or likely that does it' (Radford 1975: 240). That is, taking p to be some event, Radford's conclusion is as follows:

B: Amongst the causes of an emotion felt towards p is the belief that p is actual, or likely to be actual.

Radford supplements B with two additional claims. The first is that it is *necessary* that the relevant belief be amongst the causes: 'what is necessary in other contexts [that is, contexts other than fictional contexts], *viz.*, belief...' (Radford 1975: 247–8, 245). The second is that by 'actual' is not restricted to p occurring or being likely to occur in the environment of the person feeling the emotion. He requires only that p is or has been actual at some place and some time: 'there is no problem with being moved by historical novels or plays, documentary films etc.' (Radford 1975: 240). Incorporating these two claims, we have the conclusion for which Radford argues:

C: Amongst the causes of an emotion felt towards p, it is necessary that there be a belief that p is actual, or likely to be actual, or has been actual.

Radford's next step is to point out that, as a matter of fact, we do feel emotions towards events that feature fictional characters: 'We weep, we pity Anna Karenina, we blink hard when Mercutio is dying...' (Radford 1975: 241). On the assumption that we believe we are reading fiction, the belief that these characters are actual or have been actual is not part of the cause of these emotions. Furthermore, it is not the case that the events that feature these characters are likely to be actual as, by 'likely to be actual', Radford means something like 'Given the actual state of the world now, is p likely to occur' (Radford 1975: cf. 244).

Hence, there is a problem. Radford accepts the truth of C but also accepts some counter-examples to C (in short, he accepts that it is not the case that C). He then goes on to canvas a number of 'solutions' to the problem. The bulk of these attempt to show that, despite appearances, the relevant belief is amongst the causes of our emotions felt towards events that feature fictional characters or that the events that feature fictional characters are not the objects of our emotions. As none of these solutions has commanded widespread acceptance (least of all by Radford) I shall ignore them. Faced with an apparent contradiction, Radford concludes that, in feeling emotions for fictional characters, we are being 'inconsistent' (Radford 1975: 248).

The most obvious problem in Radford's account is that he cannot hold both C and that it is not the case that C. It does not help to say that we are inconsistent; that is akin to saying that, as we cannot be in two places at one, we are being inconsistent when we do. Furthermore, Radford's argument is not sufficient to establish C. He argues from examples which all have the following form. Find some scenario in which an emotion causally depends on an existence claim, remove the existence claim, and note that the emotion disappears with it. He then concludes that necessarily, amongst the causes of emotions are existence claims. This is akin to proving that all fires are caused by lightning strikes by finding some scenario in which a fire depends on a lightning strike, removing the lightning strike, and noting that the fire disappears with it. What is neglected in each case is the possibility of scenarios in which the effect appears without that particular kind of cause.

Radford might argue that the role of the examples was not to establish C, but rather to soften us up into accepting the intuitive truth of C. Is C intuitively acceptable? C claims rather that emotions, all emotions, necessarily have, amongst their causes, a belief as to the actuality, probability, or past actuality of their objects. It is difficult to see that C has *any* intuitive appeal. C entails that it is impossible to feel emotions towards any future events that are not immediately probable, that emotions cannot be part of any hypothetical reasoning, and that emotions cannot be part of our engagement with fictions. Not only are these claims outlandish, but Radford himself provides us with counterexamples to them. There is a sensible distinction to be drawn somewhere here (of which more later) although Radford fails to draw it.

Although Radford's arguments are directed towards C, one might think he has confused 'causally necessary' with 'conceptually necessary'. That is, that he has confused the resolutely causal claim C with the following conceptual claim.

D: Necessarily, an emotion incorporates an existential belief about its object.

That is, however emotion-like a state is, if it lacks an existential belief about its object, it is not an emotion. This too would generate puzzles about emotions felt for events that feature fictional characters, as we lack existential beliefs about such characters. This is no comfort for Radford, however, as this is subject to the same counter-examples at C. Once again, it would be impossible to feel emotions towards future events, emotions could not be part of any hypothetical reasoning, and emotions could not be part of our engagement with fictions. I mention the possibility of confusion as the absence of clarity as to whether the issue is the truth of C or the truth of D has bedevilled this debate.

This brings us directly to the vast literature that followed Radford's paper on the so-called 'paradox of fiction'. The paradox is most often stated as an apparently inconsistent triad with a version of either C or D as the middle proposition. Here is a version by Gregory Currie:

The problem is given by the existence of three plausible but mutually contradictory propositions:
(1) We have emotions concerning the situations of fictional characters.
(2) To have an emotion concerning someone's situation we must believe the propositions that describe that situation.
(3) We do not believe the propositions that describe the situations of fictional characters.
Asserting all three propositions will land us in contradiction, resolvable by denying any one of the three. The problem is to decide which one, and further, to decide what to replace it with. (Currie 1990: 187)

Other versions of (2) have been given by Jerrold Levinson ('How can we coherently have emotions for fictional persons or situations, given that we do not believe in their existence' (Levinson 1997: 38)[2]) and Peter Lamarque and Stein Olsen ('A necessary condition for experiencing emotions such as fear, pity, desire, etc. is that those experiencing them believe the objects of their emotions to exist' (Lamarque and Olsen 2004: 298)). On no occasion do any of these philosophers cite any source for this view or mention any

---

[2] The quotation is from the reprint. The original was interestingly different: 'Emotions for objects logically presuppose beliefs in the existence and features of those objects' (Levinson 1997: 23).

philosopher who has held this view. A philosopher who is more careful on this point is Alex Neill who, although he does not subscribe to a version of (2), finds its sources in the (so-called) 'cognitive theory of the emotions' (specifically in Anthony Kenny and William Lyons) (Neill 1993: 264, 265).

Putting aside various historical antecedents, the cognitive theory of the emotions emerged in the late 1950s as a reaction against theories that identified emotions with either mental or bodily feelings. It argued that emotions are caused by, and identified by, their cognitive component. What makes something an instance of fear is neither a feeling of anxiety nor a fluttering heart, but some pro-attitude to the proposition (say) that one is threatened. As the standard pro-attitude to a proposition is belief, it is understandable that belief was the mental state that tended to be mentioned. However, if one considers the two distinctions a cognitive theory needs to make (to distinguish itself from 'feeling' theories and to distinguish those that have an emotion from those that do not) it does not require belief: it only requires some pro-attitude or other (which could be a belief, an evaluation, a positive appraisal, or even an imagined state). Indeed, when one looks at those theorists to whom Neill directs us one finds this is exactly the case. Kenny's theory is elusive, but certainly does not imply anything as strong as C or D. Lyons summarizes the cognitive theory in a way that falls far short of C or D: 'a cognitive theory of emotions is one that makes some aspect of thought, usually a belief, central to the concept of emotion and, at least in some cognitive theories, essential to distinguishing different emotions from one another'(Lyons 1980: 33). Lyons' own theory is in terms of 'evaluative judgements' and he explicitly allows that emotions can be had in the absence of beliefs (Lyons 1980: 73–7). If we cannot find support for C or D in philosophers writing at a time in which the cognitive theory was dominant, still less can we find it in philosophers since. At least since Patricia Greenspan's *Emotions and Reasons* (Greenspan 1988) philosophers writing on the emotions regularly disavow the claim that beliefs are either causally or conceptually necessary for the emotions. As usually stated, the paradox of fiction is as made from straw as a man can be.

Despite the fact that Radford's arguments were flawed and his conclusions false, his paper had the effect of convincing some that there really was a problem in this area. Hence, the ground was prepared for Kendall Walton's paper, 'Fearing Fictions' which came out three years later (Walton 1978). To anticipate, Walton's arguments were not flawed and his conclusion was not false. The problem, in terms of making sense of the debate, is that he had no interest in either C or D; he was arguing for a different point altogether. It is misleading to bring Walton's paper and Radford's paper under the single heading of 'the paradox of fiction'. As Walton's 1978 paper has been superseded by the discussion in *Mimesis as Make-Believe*, I will focus on that.

Walton introduces his discussion through an example with which his name seems indelibly associated.

> Charles is watching a horror movie about a terrible green slime. He cringes in his seat as the slime oozes slowly but relentlessly over the earth, destroying everything in its path. Soon a greasy head emerges from the undulating mass, and two beady eyes fix on the camera. The slime, picking up speed, oozes on a new course straight toward the viewers. Charles emits a shriek and clutches desperately at his chair. Afterwards, still shaken, he confesses that he was 'terrified' of the slime. (Walton 1990: 196)

The problem this poses is that Charles is fully aware that he is not threatened by the slime, as he is aware that he is watching a representation (indeed, a fictional representation). Walton is proposing something like the following claim:

> E: Some emotions felt for oneself necessarily involve a belief in the possibility of interaction between oneself and the object of the emotion.

That is, Charles cannot fear being harmed by the slime unless he believes it is possible that he will be harmed by the slime. Consider the example of cowboys and Indians, and some child—Freddie—who has been charged with 'defending the fort' and is excitedly watching in case some children dressed in feathered headdresses come charging across the grass. Freddie reports that he is 'terrified of attack by Indians'. It would be a mistake to describe Freddie as being 'terrified'. One would be rightly criticized if one answered Freddie's mother's question—'How is Freddie getting on?'—with the answer 'He is terrified'. That would override a perfectly sensible distinction; the correct answer is that he is enjoying himself, being 'terrified in the game'. The first answer would alarm Freddie's mother, the second would reassure her. Unlike C or D, E seems to be true.

The solution to the problem posed by the conjunction of E and Charles's claim that he is terrified follows easily from Walton's overall account. There is a game of make-believe in which Charles is a prop for himself and the image on the screen is a prop for the slime. Although it is not true in the actual world that it is possible that Charles be harmed by the slime it is 'make-believe true' that it is possible that Charles be harmed by the slime: 'He is an actor, of a sort, in his game, as well as an object; he is a reflexive prop generating fictional truths about himself' (Walton 1990: 242). What goes on in the make-believe mimics what would go on in the actual world. Charles realizes that fictionally the slime threatens him. This realization causes a 'physiological-psychological state' in Charles: 'His muscles are tensed, he clutches his chair, his pulse quickens, his adrenaline flows' (Walton 1990: 196). Walton calls this state 'quasi-fear'. In the actual world, there is a cognitive component (the realization of it being fictionally the case that Charles is threatened) plus whatever else goes to make up an emotion. The fact that this is true of Charles in the actual world makes it fictional of Charles that he fears for himself. Thus it is not actual that Charles fears for himself, it is fictional that Charles fears for himself. That is, it follows from Walton's account that we discriminate between emotions and emotions-felt-within-the-game. Walton's account has the resources to supply such a discrimination. In short, it follows from Walton's account that there is a problem, and the account supplies the solution. Walton does not need to do any extra work to 'fill the gap' left by the denial that we can fear for ourselves in fictional scenarios; as he says, 'What fills the gap is something we have on hand anyway' (Walton 1990: 249).

I shall mention, only to put aside, two criticisms of Walton that can be found in the literature as they are apt to confuse matters. The first can be found in Noel Carroll's *The Philosophy of Horror*:

The key objection to Walton's theory, of course, is that it relegates our emotional responses to fiction to the realm of make-believe. Purportedly, when we recoil with apparent emotion to *The Exorcist*, we are only pretending to be horrified. But I, at least, recall being genuinely horrified by the film. (Carroll 1990: 73–4)

The exact nature of this criticism is unclear. I shall divide it into two. First, that Walton's account does not do justice to the phenomenology of the feelings we have towards fictional characters; second, that it does not do justice to the involuntariness of such feelings[3]. These objections are easily dealt with. There is nothing in Walton's account to suggest that the feelings

---

[3] This is considered as an additional problem by Carroll, but for ease of exposition I will consider both together.

we have towards fictional characters are somehow phenomenologically deficient; indeed, it is intrinsic to his theory that fictional world emotions will be similar in quality and could be similar in vivacity to actual world emotions.[4] Second, involuntariness plays no part in Walton's account. The image on the screen changes, which causes Charles to register that (it is make-believe that) the slime is oozing towards him, which causes the reaction of quasi-fear. No stage of this is a matter of choice. Walton himself has stated: 'It goes without saying that we *are* genuinely moved by novels and films and plays, that we respond to works of fiction with real emotion' (Walton 1997: 38). Any objection based on the charge that Walton's account somehow 'downgrades' emotions felt for fictional characters is mistaken. The second criticism is that Walton's view is motivated by an adherence to some version of the cognitive theory of the emotions. Once again, Walton is explicit that this is not the case.[5] As is clear from the above quotation he thinks we feel 'genuine emotions' towards events featuring fictional characters in the absence of belief, and furthermore he clearly states that we can feel emotions towards actual objects and events in the absence of belief (Walton 1990: 245).

Problems only emerge for Walton when he generalizes his account from emotions felt for oneself to emotions felt for other people.

Fictionally one may fear for someone else, if not for oneself. A spectator of the shower scene in Hitchcock's *Psycho* probably does not take himself to be in danger or fear for himself. Fictionally, he is aware of danger to someone else (a character played by Janet Leigh), and his shrieks are fictionally shrieks of fear for her. (Walton 1990: 250)

Walton would be on strong ground if he argued for this generalization only after establishing the truth of his overall account as—as he rightly points out—his overall account has the resources to provide a solution. However, he does not; he builds the generalization into his statement of the problem which, he will claim, provides independent support for his overall account as it is able to provide a solution. That is, one would only agree that Walton had a solution to this problem if one already agreed his account was correct. Here is his initial statement of the problem (which we first met in Chapter 2).

---

[4] This was pointed out by Malcolm Budd as early as 1985 (Budd 1985: 130).
[5] Walton is usually taken to deny (1) of the inconsistent triad given earlier. It would be more accurate—although still inaccurate—to hold that he denies (2).

To allow that mere fictions are the objects of our psychological attitudes while dis-allowing the possibility of physical interaction severs the normal links between the physical and the psychological. What is pity or anger which is never to be acted on? What is love that cannot be expressed to its object and it logically or metaphysi-cally incapable of consummation? We cannot even try to rescue Robinson Crusoe from his island, not matter how deep our concern for him. (Walton 1990: 196)

This seeks to establish the following claim:

F: Emotions felt for others necessarily involve the possibility of interaction between oneself and the object of the emotion.

Unlike E, F lacks credibility. If it were the case then emotions would be absent in all situations in which we lacked instrumental beliefs (beliefs about the means by which we can act on our desires). We would be mis-taken in thinking that we can feel emotions in any representation relation, including representations of events distant in time, space, or both time and space. That seems absurd; if I can feel sorry for anyone, I can surely feel sorry for the poor bloody infantry slogging it out during the Battle of the Somme. As Walton fails to establish F, he provides no independ-ent reason to reject the claim that, amongst the responses we have when engaging with narratives, non-fictional or fictional, will be emotions felt for other people.

Whether we consider the problem to be one of emotions felt for oneself or emotions felt for other people, Walton's discussion of our psychologi-cal participation with fictional worlds inherits the problem identified in Chapter 2. That is, the class of works picked out by what we are mandated to imagine is broader than that traditionally classified as fiction: indeed, it is the class of representations (at least, all but the thinnest representa-tions). The independent attempts to motivate problems rest on the pos-sibility or impossibility of interaction. As should now be familiar, he does not divide non-fictions from fictions but confrontation relations from representation relations. In the case of E, the scenario Walton provides for Charles can easily be restated with a non-fictional example. In a docu-mentary on creatures from the deep, the great white shark suddenly turns and snaps at the cage from which it is being filmed. Once again, as the gaping jaws fill the screen, 'Charles emits a shriek and clutches desperately at his chair'. Charles no more believes there is a possibility of interaction between himself and the actual shark then he believes there is an interac-tion between himself and the fictional slime. The case of F is even more straightforward. If the problem is emotions that take place without 'the possibility of physical interaction', then this applies to all representations, whether non-fictional or fictional. Hence, whichever way it is approached, whatever problem Walton has identified, is not a problem for fictions but a problem for representations.

Aside from the incompatibility between E and Charles' claim to be terrified (to which I return below) are there *any* arguments for the traditional 'paradox of fiction'? It might be thought that there is a problem with the objects of the emotion: namely, that in actual cases there is an object to be pitied and in fictional cases there is not. We could state the contrast as follows. The answer to the question 'Who is it that you pity?' is, in the case of Cleopatra, a simple one: I pity Cleopatra. We cannot give an analogous answer in the case of Anna Karenina as there is no Anna Karenina.

Let us assume, then, that 'pities' takes a direct object. As 'pities' is a psychological verb, and generates an opaque context, it is one of the so-called 'intensional transitives' (Forbes 2006: ch. 3). If the problem would be solved by finding something that play the same role as Cleopatra would in the historical case, we would need to show that Anna was in fact an object—of an albeit peculiar sort. Realist views of the ontology of fictional characters are that they are real and non-existent (Meinongianism); real but non-actual (inhabitants of Lewisean possible worlds); or real but not-concrete (abstracta). Although these views have had able defenders, they appear to face insuperable difficulties.[6]

Alternatively, we could give up realism about fictional characters, and show that the relevant verbs are not transitive after all. One option would be to embrace propositionalism: we replace what appears to be an attitude to an object (our feeling pity towards X) with an attitude to a proposition (our feeling pity that p). Our case would be analogous to the following. It looks as if 'Ernest is hunting a lion' entails the existence of a lion. However, if we read the sentence as 'Ernest is endeavouring that Ernest shoots a lion' this does not entail the existence of a lion (Quine 1960: 154).[7] There are, however, two objections to making this move. The first is that our attitude

---

[6] See (Sainsbury 2010: ch. 2–6). Realists would be justified in complaining an inadequate dismissal of their position. In mitigation, the view for which I will argue sidesteps this debate, and therefore it is not one on which I need take a view.

[7] This is Mark Sainsbury's solution, and possibly also that of Peter Lamarque (Lamarque 1981 and Lamarque and Olsen 1994: 101–6).

appears to be *de re* and not *de dicto*; we might *regret* that Cleopatra is hounded to her death, or *regret* that that Anna was scorned, but our *pity* is for the particular people involved (this problem is not solved by ensuring that the proposition picks out a unique individual (Lamarque and Olsen 1994: 103)). Second, propositionalism hides the problem, it does not solve it. The problem is not primarily the fact that Anna does not exist but that (putting the point in propositionalist terms) our regret that Anna was scorned makes no sense given that we believe that nobody was scorned. If our problem is with Ernest hunting a lion given that he believes that there are no lions, then our problem is not solved by claiming that what is actually going on is that Ernest is endeavouring that Ernest shoots a lion.

It is worth a brief digression to point out that those who think this is the problem are not helped by the position Walton takes in chapters 6 and 7 of *Mimesis as Make-Believe*. That is, being prompted by the written word to imagine that certain states of affairs obtain does not introduce an object for our psychological attitudes. The analogy he draws with children's games of make-believe can encourage a misreading.

What, then, is the point of imagining the stump to be a bear? Why not simply imagine a bear in the path? How does the stump's role as an object of imagination, not just a prompter, contribute to the imaginative experience? An intuitive answer is that the stump 'gives substance,' as we might describe it, to the imaginary bear. When the stump is imagined to be a bear, there *is* something—something real and solid and kickable—which can be called the imaginary bear. No such substantial object can be identified as the imaginary bear when one merely imagines a bear at a certain spot. I believe that this difference partly accounts for the impression which I have, and which I suspect others share, that an experience of imagining a bear is likely to be more 'vivid' if one imagines of some actual object that it is a bear than if one does not. (Walton 1990: 26).

The object of our fear within the game is not (of course) the stump but the bear, and there is no bear. The stump, however, can be the focus for our attitude. We do not have even this when reading fiction. The text of *Anna Karenina* prompts us to believe that it is make-believe the case that Anna is unhappy, that this prompts feelings of quasi-pity which makes it make-believe the case that we pity Anna. Thus, within the 'game world' of reading the book, we can truly say things such as 'I pity Anna' or, as is more likely, express our sympathy for Anna. Furthermore, we not only imagine that we pity Anna, we imagine pitying her 'from the inside' (Walton 1990: 247). However, none of this generates Anna as an object for our pity. Indeed, Walton is an irrealist; that is, he does not think that there are objects, or need be objects, of our psychological attitudes to fictional characters. Hence the answer he provides to the issue of the absent object comes only in chapter 10, where he considers fictional ontology.

We are wading into murky issues of semantics, reference, and mental intentionality. If the realists are right, the semantics of fictional discourse will require that a referent such that 'Anna Karenina' refers to Anna Karenina analogously to the way in which 'Cleopatra' refers to Cleopatra. However, I doubt that is what is at issue here. To see this, let us return to our example of a confrontation relation: a situation which has the possibility of action built into it. Three wolves run into the cave and attack. I run for the axe, Johnnie runs for help, and Katie tries to scare them off with fire. In this case there are objects in our immediate environment which are those objects on which our attention is directed, our emotions are directed, and which form the locus of our actions. The package makes sense: the objects, the psychological state, and the actions form a coherent whole. In a representation relation, the object is absent: there is nothing—no Anna Karenina but no Cleopatra either—which forms the focus of our attention, emotion, and action. In short, in terms of an object on which our attention and emotion is focused the contrast is exactly where my view claims it to be: between a confrontation relation and a representation relation. Of course, in a representation relation an object has to be somehow introduced as the object of our attention. However, this is—obviously—as much a problem for our psychological participation with non-fictional representations as it is for fictional representations.

In short, there is an issue as to whether or not the objects of emotions are actual. However, the issue is whether the objects of the emotions are actually there or whether they are not actually there. Radford had a point until he blithely slipped in (without argument) that 'there is no problem about being moved by historical novels or plays, documentary films, etc.' (Radford 1975: 240). Those still tempted to think what matters is whether the object *ever* existed, should contrast the confrontation relation I have just described with two other situations. In the first, I gather my family together and talk them through what happened twenty years ago when my grandfather was attacked by wolves. I make it clear to them that I am telling them about something that actually happened, and tell them, in bloodcurdling detail, how the wolves operated; one of them went left, the other one went right, and the third never left the opening of the cave. Alternatively, rather than telling of an actual incident, I could talk them through some story I have made up. I make it clear to them that what I am telling them did not actually happen but, as I am an expert on wolf attacks, I am able to give a credible and bloodcurdling account of how three wolves would attack; one would go left, one could go right, and the third would never leave the opening of the cave. In both of these two latter situations no object is present, and yet both involve emotions directed upon objects. Some account of this needs to be given, but the account is needed for both the non-fictional and the fictional story.

This is not the place to embark on an account of intentional objects. I am content to have shown that no version of the so-called 'paradox of fiction' re-instates the non-fiction/fiction contrast as fundamental, and that the problem is a particular case of a larger question which can be settled elsewhere. I will, however, say something about one view of intentional objects, as, if it is right, it would straightforwardly reintroduce the contrast between non-fictional and fictional objects. This is the view that *intentionality* is a relation between thought and some actual object. In the case of Cleopatra the object is Cleopatra; what the object is in the case of Anna is unclear. In short, if intentionality is a relation between a thought and some actual object, the appeal to intentional objects would simply reintroduce our problem. This is John Searle's view:

> ...an Intentional object is just an object like any other; it has no peculiar ontological status at all. To call something an Intentional object is just to say that it is what some intentional state is about. Thus, for example, if Bill admires President Carter, then the Intentional object of his admiration is President Carter, the actual man and not some shadowy intermediate entity between Bill and the man. (Searle 1983)

Searle's view, however, is controversial. Tim Crane has argued, surely correctly, that the view is untenable not least because the objects of our thoughts includes things that do not exist and something cannot both not exist and be 'just an object like any other' (Crane 2001). What Crane does say about intentional objects seems particularly suited to our case:

> The word 'object' has a different meaning in these phrases than it does in the phrases 'physical object', 'material object', 'mental object', and even 'abstract object'. This is the key to the idea that being an intentional object is not being a thing of any kind. For 'intentional object' in this respect (unsurprisingly) is like 'object of attention' rather than 'physical object'. (Crane 2001: 341)

According to Crane, intentional objects are not the kinds of object we have in the case of Cleopatra and lack in the case of Anna. Crane denies that there is any 'substantial conception' of intentional object in the sense that it is a part of the substantial conception of (for example) physical objects that they exist in space and time. What we would need to do would be to give a detailed account of the nature of the intentional phenomena although, as the moment, I have little idea of how to give such an account.[8]

The claim on which my account is based is that it is the function of representations to bring states of affairs into our attentional environment. They cannot bring the object itself into our attentional environment (Cleopatra has been dead for 2000 years) so they bring the situation to our attention: that is, Cleopatra as described in a certain way. This is the object of our attention and the object of our emotions. The same is true of Anna. The difference between the two is that Cleopatra's situation occurred in the past of the actual world and Anna's did not, but this is not a difference that makes a difference. That point—that psychological participation in all representations, whether fiction or non-fiction, merit the same treatment—has been made by Richard Gerrig.

Consider the beginning of a firsthand account of the storming of the Winter Palace in St. Petersburg on November 7, 1917, written by the journalist John Reed:

> Like a black river, filling all the street, without song or cheer we poured through the Red Arch, where the man just ahead of me said in a low voice, 'Look out, comrades! Don't trust them. They will fire, surely!' In the open we began to run, stooping low and bunching together, and jammed up suddenly behind the pedestal of the Alexander Column.

As with the newspaper articles, readers (presumably) believe that Reed's utterances were intended to be felicitous in the context in which they were uttered. Once again, however, readers must come to an understanding of these utterances in circumstances well removed from that context. Reed, like authors of fiction, is informing us about a world to which we have no immediate access. This is no less true because the world in question was, at one time, real. (Gerrig 1993: 130–1)

The fundamental contrast, once again, is between confrontations and representations. In a confrontation, the object of our emotion is the thing, or the state of affairs, before our eyes. With a representation, there is no such thing or state of affairs. We construct a mental model from the

---

[8] Crane's book, *The Objects of Thought* (OUP, 2013), was published too recently for me to take it into account.

representation, and amongst the p-responses we have towards this content will be emotions felt towards characters in the representation.

Although we have succeeded in demonstrating the absence of reasons to think there is a problem with emotions felt for fictional characters, we are still left with Walton's initial problem: that we appear to have, in representation relations, emotions that properly belong in confrontation relations. I confess to be slightly unsettled by Charles-like cases. However, there are reasons for thinking that they are unusual. Walton's example depends on an 'aside to the audience'; that is, the slime looks at and comes oozing towards Charles.[9] One might take the view that asides ('breaking the fourth wall') are violations of the conventions (or the structure, or the logic) of representation. Walton's view, which follows from our being reflexive props within the fiction, is that asides are intrinsic to engaging with representations, and he has special 'error theories' as to why they appear anomalous (Walton 1990: 229–37). Even if we are persuaded by Walton on this—and I am not sure we should be—it is unusual for an aside to be threatening rather than merely a means of imparting information. This suggests at least attempting to find an account that can accommodate the usual cases and explain emotions felt for ourselves as a special case.

There is an alternative explanation that does not require that we take seriously Charles' claim that he was terrified. Noel Carroll has pointed out that films are particularly adept at exploiting our non-rational responses.

Theater and perhaps especially film exploit our affective reflexes for artistic effect mercilessly. In staging a theatrical thriller like *The Lady in Black*, a white face pops out of the dark in a way that induces us to jump out of our seats, as do sudden explosions, fast movements toward the camera, and the offscreen rumblings and screams in so many films, implemented by awesome surround-sound systems of ever increasing magnitude, realism, and complexity. If these effects in cinema sometimes prompt us to start upward, careening cameras encourage us to hold onto our seats for dear life. Manipulating such variables as speed, scale, lighting, and sound, among others, the filmmaker often appears to have direct access to our nervous system, bypassing the cerebral cortex and triggering automatic affective reflexes. (Carroll 2003: 524)

---

[9] Walton rightly points out that an aside is not necessary: 'it can be fictional that one is in danger without it being fictional that one is noticed' (Walton 1990: 250). However, all such cases depend upon possibility of the 'fourth wall' being broken, which is a violation of convention.

What Charles describes as 'being terrified' simply could be a vivid way of expressing the fact that he was shocked (an a-rational response therefore requiring no explanation in terms of objects) by a 'fast movement towards the camera'. If this were the case, then Charles would not believe that it was make-believe the case that he was threatened (indeed, he would have no beliefs about the nature of the spatial relation between him and the slime). Rather, he would be involuntarily startled by a sudden and surprising turn of events on the screen.[10]

One consideration in support of this is that it is difficult to envisage Charles-like cases occurring away from depictive representations. The usual examples of 'asides' from within a book do not prompt emotions felt for ourselves; instead they prompt an emotion felt for the fictional narrator. There are, of course, instances of emotions felt for oneself which take as objects actual tokens of a type encountered in a representation. For example, reading a narrative about sadistic housebreakers might make us fear actual sadistic housebreakers. That, however, is simply a case of worrying about what might happen and requires no special explanation. The special powers of cognitive affect enjoyed by depictive representations lend support to Carroll's explanation of the case.

In summary, I have attempted to disentangle the various issues involved in the 'paradox of fiction'. The problem is independent of whether we think emotions require beliefs and independent of whether the object of the emotion is fictional. Rather, the problem—if there is a problem—turns out to be the familiar problem of intentional objects. This does not accommodate Charles-like cases. Fortunately the appearance of the problem there can be explained away. Having, I hope, put to rest doubts that my approach cannot address a central issue in the (so-called) philosophy of fiction, let us press on to consider three further problems discussed in that branch of the subject.

[10] This suggestion is now the standard 'non-Waltonian' solution to E in the literature (a good statement of it can be found in Choi (2003)). It was first made, as far as I know, in Neill (1991: 55).

9

Narrators, Impossible fictions, and the 'Fictionality Puzzle'

In this chapter I will consider three further debates that have raged within the contemporary philosophy of fiction.

Narrators

I have argued that our engagement with narratives is neutral between them being non-fictional and them being fictional. This throws the debate about the existence or not of ubiquitous fictional narrators into a new light although (perhaps surprisingly) much of the existing debate continues to be relevant.

I shall assume that all narratives (non-fiction and fiction) are created by someone; there is a flesh-and-blood author. As we have seen, Walton denies this: he maintains that something can be a representation, regardless of the intentions of its maker, 'if things of that kind are typically or normally meant by their makers to serve that purpose' (Walton 1990: 52). I shall ignore this complication. The flesh-and-blood author is the actual entity who produces the narrative—an entity I shall from now on call 'the actual author'. Jerrold Levinson and others have argued that it is not the actual author who is relevant to criticism, but 'the implied author': the author as manifest in the narrative. The most illuminating way to think of the implied author is as an entity constructed out of our engaging with the narrative. According to Levinson,

> . . . the core of literary meaning, as with any piece of discourse publicly presented, is not the meaning (the many meanings) of the words and sentences taken in abstraction from the author, or precisely of necessity the meaning that the actual author intended to put across, but our best *hypothetical attribution* of such, formed from the position of the intended audience. (Levinson 1992: 179)[1]

---

[1] The position Levinson articulates here does not entail the implied author. Indeed, Levinson's view is that we hypothesize the intentions of the actual author. I have no strong

Our 'best hypothetical attributions' might result in a set of intentions that were not precisely those of the actual author. Instead, we attribute those intentions to a construct: the implied author.

Throughout his paper (indeed, in the above quotation) Levinson talks of 'literature', 'literary meaning', and 'literary texts'. Hence, it is unclear whether he restricts his claim to fiction or whether he thinks it applies generally to fiction and non-fiction. It would seem he is committed to the latter. His is a thesis about meaning of a passage of words: in the case of fiction, the meaning of a passage is given by our best hypothetical attribution of the meaning the author intended to put across. It is unclear why the same passage of words, were it a non-fiction, should have its meaning determined in a different way. Neither might capture what the actual author intended—but that is exactly Levinson's point. Hence, with both fictional and non-fictional narratives we have both an actual author and an implied author.

Next up is the narrator who is explicit in the text. Once again, such a narrator appears in both non-fictional and fictional works. Unlike fictional explicit narrators, non-fictional explicit narrators are rarely given the task of narrating the whole story. Chaucer's pilgrims, Conrad's Marlow, and Conan Doyle's Dr Watson tell us the tale from beginning to end. William Dalrymple, in *Return of a King* (his account of Imperial adventures in nineteenth-century Afghanistan) only occasionally hands over the narrative to the contemporary chronicler, Mirza 'Ata. There is no reason why non-fictional explicit narrators should not take centre stage, however. One could easily imagine a denizen of the hotel bar in Kubri in 1917 beginning a narrative describing T.E. Lawrence's appearance (in the 'Staff uniform of the Sherif of Mecca' (Lawrence 1939: 327)), before simply reporting Lawrence's verbal account of the fall of Akaba.

The philosophical controversy concerns the need for 'effaced', or 'elusive' narrators. That is, the question is whether we need narrators for all narratives, including narratives that do not feature explicit narrators.[2] Let

views on the matter, but in what follows I shall assume the view that criticism requires an implied author (Booth 1991).

[2] This is not quite right, as proponents of the view generally allow that some fictional narratives do not have effaced narrators (exceptions are Seymour Chatman and my former self (Chatman 1990: 109–23; Matravers 1997)). I shall ignore this complication. Prominent proponents of effaced narrators are Jerrold Levinson and George M. Wilson (Levinson 1996; Wilson 2011). Critics include Alex Byrne, Noel Carroll, Andrew Kania, Gregory Currie,

us put the unproblematic facts of the matter to one side. Every narrative is constructed by some actual narrator. The actual narrator will usually have a purpose in so doing, whether that be entertainment, instruction, edification, or something else. The question is whether, in addition to such a metaphysically unproblematic person, we need a further narrator who stands in a different relation to the narrative.

The strongest form of argument for effaced narrators takes them to be implied by the nature of our engagement with fictional narratives. There are other arguments, but I take them to have been dealt with sufficiently elsewhere (see in particular, Currie (2010)). I am going to consider two arguments for the claim that *fictional* works require effaced narrators. The success of either of these arguments would be bad news for my project, as it would imply that our engagement with fictional narratives differs in at least this way from our engagement with non-fictional narratives.

The first is from David Lewis. Here is Lewis 'first approximation' as to the content of fiction:

> What is true in the Sherlock Holmes stories would then be what is true at all of those possible worlds where there are characters who have the attributes, stand in the relations, and do the deeds that are ascribed in the stories to Holmes, Watson, and the rest. (Lewis 1978: 39)

It is possible, however, that by massive coincidence there are in the actual world characters called 'Holmes', 'Watson', and so on, who did exactly those things described in the stories. However, it is false that in the actual world 'Sherlock Holmes' would refer to that person. In short, Lewis needs to find a way of ruling out the actual world. He does this, as we saw in the Chapter 6, by constraining the world under consideration to those in which the fiction 'is told as known fact'. This argument works only if one accepts Lewis' account of the content of fiction, which in turn would mean accepting Lewis' account of possible worlds and reference across worlds. I do not have a view on this so shall put it to one side. Lewis' argument does not stem from considerations of the reader's engagement with narratives; indeed, it is worth remembering that he described it as an 'artificial dodge to meet a technical difficulty' (Lewis 1978: 276).

Berys Gaut, and David Davies (Byrne 1993; Kania 2005; Carroll 2006; Currie 2010: 65–85; Davies 2010; Gaut 2011). Walton, although often cited as a proponent, seems to me to not really take sides (Walton 1990: 365).

The next argument deserves more lengthy consideration: it is what Andrew Kania has called 'the ontological gap' argument—which he attributes to Jerrold Levinson (Kania 2005: 48). The argument has two steps. For the moment, I shall simply state the first step; I shall return to it for detailed consideration shortly. Seymour Chatman puts the point in its simplest form: 'every narrative is by definition narrated' (Chatman 1990: 115). If the narrative is narrated, then there is a narrator. Levinson then argues that, if we need such a narrator, he or she will be on the fictional rather than the actual side of the divide (Levinson is considering depictive rather than verbal representations, but the point generalizes).

A narrator and the events narrated by the narrator must be on the same fictional plane, otherwise cognitive relations posited between the narrator and events would not make sense. The cinematic narrator's logical status vis-à-vis the film is to be distinguished from the narrator's degree of involvement—causal, emotional, experiential—in the story, i.e. what literary theorists mark as the narrators being either homodiegetic or heterodiegetic. Being heterodiegetic, or an 'outsider' to the events being related, does not remove a filmic narrator ontologically from the characters he/she/it serves to offer us perceptual access to…the narrator must perforce share the fictional plane of the characters, since they are apparently real and reportable to the narrator, and this is true whether the narrator is homodiegetic, i.e. involved in the story events, or heterodiegetic, i.e. uninvolved in them, standing to those events merely in a witnessing and transmitting capacity. (Levinson 1996: 149–50)

Let us consider an example. The following is a passage from Muriel Spark's novel, *The Prime of Miss Jean Brodie*:

These girls formed the Brodie set. That was what they had been called even before the headmistress had given them the name, in scorn, when they had moved from the Junior to the Senior school at the age of twelve. At that time they had been immediately recognizable as Miss Brodie's pupils, being vastly informed on a lot of subjects irrelevant to the authorized curriculum, as the headmistress said, and useless to the school as a school. (Spark 1961: 1)

Levinson's point is that the reader is to imagine the events described in this passage are true. That is, the reader is to imagine that they are given to us as true. If being given to us implies that there is a giver, the giver gives them to us as true. If the giver gives them to us as true, the giver believes them. Thus, the giver is not the actual or implied author, as the actual or implied author does not believe them. Hence, the conclusion: 'the narrator must perforce share the fictional plane of the characters'.

Levinson's argument has been the subject of much criticism. Here, for example, is Noel Carroll. Carroll disputes Levinson's construal of the reader's engagement with the text (his example comes from the film, *The Way We Were*).

> If signalling that such-and-such is fictional instructs the audience to imagine it as true, why isn't the fictive intention of the author (that we imagine such-and-such) adequate to warrant supposing that such-and-such is true in the fictional world? Maybe it will be said that if such-and-such is asserted, there must be an agency doing the asserting. But is 'that Katie loves Hubble' a genuine assertion? 'It is true in the fiction that "Katie loves Hubble"' is an assertion; but is 'that Katie loves Hubble' really an assertion, or merely a propositional content? (Carroll 2006: 176)

On this construal, the flesh and blood author puts p forward as 'a propositional content' intending that the reader imagine that p. There are no assertions, even within the scope of the make-believe, and hence no reason to postulate an agency doing the asserting.

The objection is that the reader can imagine the propositional content of the fiction, on the grounds of being intended to do so by the actual or implied author. Levinson's opponents might grant to him that, were there a need for an 'extra' narrator, he or she would come out on the fictional side of the divide. However—the argument goes—there is no need for such a narrator.

What, then, is Levinson's argument for a narrator? He says this:

> The presenter in a film presents, or gives perceptual access to, the story's sights and sounds; the presenter in a film is thus, in part, a sort of *perceptual enabler*. Such perceptual enabling is what we must implicitly posit to explain how it is we are, even imaginarily, perceiving what we are perceiving in the story, in the manner and order in which we are perceiving it. The notion of a presenter, whose main charge is the providing of perceptual access on the fictional world, is simply the best default assumption available for how we make sense of a narrative fiction film. (Levinson 1996: 148)

This echoes an argument for fictional narrators that Walton presents for verbal depictions in *Mimesis as Make-Believe*: 'we are so used to declarative sentences being employed to report events and describe people and situations that, when we experience a literary work, we almost inevitably imagine someone using or having used its sentences thus' (Walton 1990: 265).

George Wilson has recently made some sensible remarks about this debate. The dispute 'turns chiefly on what constitutes the preferred description of the phenomenology of our imaginative engagement with

novels and kindred fictions'. As he points out, 'it is not obvious how a dispute of this sort is going to get resolved' (Wilson 2011: 117). In as much
as my contribution is worth anything, it seems to me the advantage lies
with Levinson. His opponents point to the undoubted fact that the actual
or implied author presents to the reader a story to imagine. What is contained in the injunction to 'imagine a story'? Whatever the details, the
standard view is something like 'to imagine it is a report of actual events'. If
this is accepted, then Levinson's argument seems to have bite. If we are to
imagine we are being given a report of actual events, then it is not much of
a stretch to claim that this involves imagining a reporter of actual events.

George Wilson has given a further argument for the claim that engaging
with narratives entails some notion of engaging with a narrator. (Wilson's
argument is similar to another of the three arguments given by Walton for
being 'relatively liberal' in recognizing narrators (Walton 1990: 365–7).)
He engages directly with Carroll's argument cited above.

Suppose, for simplicity of formulation, that the narration of *The Way We Were*
contains the sentence 'Katie loves Hubble.' Naturally, that sentence expresses the
propositional content that Katie loves Hubble, and Carroll is opposing the idea
that this propositional content is fictionally offered as an assertion. His counter
suggestion is that readers of the novel, knowing that they are reading a work of
fiction, simply take the propositional content as something they will imagine as
part of the story.
  But, on the face of the matter, the readers will normally take this propositional
content as something that they are prescribed (defeasibly) to imagine as part of the
story only if they suppose that it is presented in the narration as having some kind
of assertive force—only if it is fictional that the propositional content is fictionally
put forward as true. Notice that in fictional narration instances of fictional assertion may predominate, but in the course of the narration, various 'propositional
contents' may be presented in a range of different modes. The propositional content 'Katie loves Hubble' may occur as merely something that some character in
the novel said or thought. Some propositional contents may be presented as having the force of a supposition, something that is merely to be entertained as possible at the pertinent juncture in the narration. Or a propositional content may be
presented as something whose truth value is being questioned. (The hypothetical
occurrence of the sentence 'Katie loves Hubble,' could be followed in the narration
by, 'Many people thought so, but was it really true?') Therefore, at a minimum, we
are going to have to draw some distinctions between the kinds of illocutionary
force that fictionally attach to the propositional contents expressed in the narration. We will need to distinguish at least between
  (4) In W, at juncture j it is fictional that it is asserted that P,
  i.e., it is fictional that P is expressed as having the force of an assertion, and

(5) In W, at juncture k, it is fictional that it is supposed that P
And
(6) In W, at juncture l, it is fictionally asked whether P,
and so on. (Wilson 2011: 119–20) cf. (Lamarque and Olsen 1994: 44)

Wilson allows that (4) to (6) may be true, and yet there still be 'no fictional *acts* of asserting, supposing and questioning'. However, he finds this 'extremely strained and artificial', and hence finds grounds for postulating a 'minimal narrating agency' (Wilson 2011: 120).

So far, I have accepted two arguments for a fictional narrator: Levinson's (or Chapman's) argument and Wilson's argument. In order to use them to bolster my own account, I need first to purge them of their misleading entanglements with fiction. The case is most obvious with Wilson, so I will begin there. The problem Wilson finds for Carroll's account does not depend on whether or not the representation is fictional. It is an entirely general question as to whether it is possible to understand a verbal representation (that is, distinguish between assertions, suppositions, questions, and so on) without taking that representation to be the product of acts of asserting, supposing, or questioning. Wilson thinks not, and I agree. Whether the representation is a non-fiction or a fiction, we have to consider it the product of (at least) a 'minimum narrating agency'.

I defended Levinson by claiming that he could borrow from what has become one of the standard views in the orthodox account. The claim—known as 'the report model'—is that what we do when we read a fiction is make-believe that we are reading a report of actual events. The motivation behind this is two-fold. First, there is a phenomenological point. When engaged with a fiction, it seems to the reader that he or she is engaging with a report about things that are happening, or have happened, elsewhere. Second, there is the explanatory point. The presupposition is that our reading non-fiction is unproblematic. Hence, if we imagine of our engaging with fiction that it is our engaging with non-fiction, we dispose of its problematic nature. Here is an analogous case. When playing cowboys and Indians, the children need a gaol. Unfortunately, they have only a length of string lying on the ground in the shape of a square which is not going to hold anyone. If they imagine of the string that it is the walls of the gaol, then the problem is solved; the string simply inherits all the unproblematic properties of the gaol.

I must confess to previously being an enthusiastic proponent of this view (Matravers 1997). However, I now think that it is wholly mistaken. Furthermore, the form of the claim should have made it fairly obvious that theft was triumphing over honest toil. One advantage with the account I now advocate is that it makes the vacuity of the move transparent. First, I will address the phenomenological point. The fundamental fact about representations, I have claimed, is that they are the means by which we learn about things that are not happening in our immediate environment. They tell us about what is happening at another place, what has happened at another place, or what could happen in another place (where the 'could' is constrained only by what we can understand). All that is relevant to the phenomenology is that the events are not happening around here and hence do not need directly to engage our motivations (although, as we have seen, representation relations can shade into confrontation relations if they enable us to infer what is likely to happen around here). The representation might be about the cave next door, the dim and distant past, or about situations that could happen but have not. That is, the representation could be set in an actual location and concern events that did not take place, or some non-actual location and concern events that did not take place. It does not seem to me to be true, and I cannot think what could be gained by it being true, that we represent the situation to ourselves as one that actually happened in some actual location (cf. Walton 1990: 84–5).

The decisive flaw in the move, however, is the presupposition that non-fictional representations are unproblematic. The only ground for this could be the thought that the problems with fiction stem from them not being about the actual world. However, as we saw in the discussion of Greg Currie's views in Chapter 3, this is not the problem: the problem is rather that of casting light on the nature of our engagement, via a representation, with events that are not happening around here. That problem is common to non-fictional and fictional representations, so we gain nothing by imagining of the latter that it is the former. All the problems concerning the relations between our knowledge sources (the text and our background knowledge), the mechanism (text-processing using our long term, short term, and working memories), our representing the situation to ourselves, and how this relates to other mental states such as our emotions (or emotion-like states) are common to both. The problem is not that we have a fiction, but that we have a representation. It is only by assuming that engaging with representations of actual events is unproblematic that we could be seduced into thinking that this move would help. That assumption enables us to escape having to deal with problems to do with fictions by assuming there are no problems to do with narratives. The shift appears to give us something for nothing, and hence its vacuity should have been obvious.

Where does this leave the question of the identity of the narrator? First we need to distinguish the facts that are external to the reader's engagement with a narrative from features of the reader's engagement with a narrative. The external facts are these: actual authors create structures of propositions which readers use to build mental models. This is done for a variety of purposes—entertainment, education, edification being only three. The creation of such structures sometimes obeys the fidelity constraint and sometimes it does not. I have argued that it is a feature of a reader's engagement that there is a 'teller of the story', a 'minimal narrating agency'. The issue as to whether he or she is or is not fictional does not arise. The claim is only that a minimal narrating agency is part of the mental model constructed by readers of both fictional and non-fictional narratives.

What does the reader take that 'minimal narrating agency' to be? There are a bewildering variety of relations between narrators and narratives: reporting and storytelling narrators, reliable and unreliable narrators, ironic narrators, and narrators that skip between the actual and the fictional realm to name only the most obvious. I shall not go into those here. Kendall Walton and Greg Currie have both done much to sort the problems out in subtle and illuminating ways to which I would have little to add (Walton 1990: ch. 9; Currie 2010: ch. 8). I will offer some thoughts on the most obvious cases.

First, there are explicit narrators. It is generally true of the Sherlock Holmes stories that Dr Watson is responsible for the Holmes narrative. Do we need to postulate a 'whoever' in addition to Dr Watson: that is, 'whoever is telling the story of Dr Watson telling the story'? Some narratives might contain features which cannot be thought of (or are not easily thought of) as the products of the explicit narrator. For example, the representation might signal that the explicit narrator is overly punctilious, and the story is too long to sustain the reader's interest. This could be done by an explicit intervention in the text: 'John Watson here exhibits that part of his personality that made him so adept at emptying the mess halls of India'. That would introduce a second narrating agency who narrates, and comments on, Dr Watson's narration. It could also be done by, say, the narrative becoming overfull of medical detail and the minutia of Watson's role in the aftermath of the Mutiny. This would not force us to postulate a second narrating agency; the reader can simply conclude, of the explicit narrator, that he is a bit of a bore. If the reader starts to detect that it is not Watson speaking, but someone caricaturing Watson speaking, then they will have detected a second narrating agency.

If there is no explicit narrator, the question as to the narrator's identity will probably not arise for the reader: the narrating agency is simply the agency to whom the reader appeals in order to distinguish assertions, suppositions, questions, and so on. In as much as the question does arise the answer will be is likely to be a definite description of the Russellian sort: 'whoever is telling the story'. The reader could go on and have further thoughts about the nature of the narrator: that he or she is witty or wise, cynical or caustic. We also engage with some narratives in order to elicit some particular person's view. In such cases we would identify the narrator with a particular person: this is not simply a story about modern America, it is Alistair Cooke's story about modern America. George Wilson has pointed out that we sometimes identify the narrator of novels with the flesh and blood author: it is Jane Austen or Muriel Spark who have settled down to tell us a story (Wilson 2011: 115).

I shall finish this section with a few remarks on the debate on (so-called) 'omniscient narrators', although I do not think my view throws new light on this debate. It is thought to be a principle—and let us leave it open what are the grounds for this principle—that if the narrator asserts something within a fiction then it is true in the fiction (we will see some important limitations on this principle below). As Kendall Walton says,

> The advantages of this arrangement are obvious. It enables the author cleanly and crisply to establish fictional truths about the characters and events described— including fictional truths about their innermost thoughts and feelings—and to provide readers sure access to them. He need only put into the mouth of his 'omniscient' narrator words expressing what he wants made fictional. (Walton 1990: 361)

The principle applies (as one would expect) to *all* narratives. The way a journalist makes some proposition true-in-the-newspaper-article is by asserting it in the article. Of course, the truth-maker of the proposition is not that it was asserted in the article; the truth-maker is (side-stepping the debate on the exact nature of truth-makers) the existence of some state of affairs in the world.

The problem is that the principle, along with the minimal narrative agency, appears to lead to absurdity. For some proposition, p, that agent can make p 'true in the story' by asserting it. As Walton says, p could describe epistemologically inaccessible states such as a person's innermost thoughts and feelings. Hence, the question could arise as to how the agent ever got him or herself into a position where they were able to assert p? In short, how could they know?

There are some narratives for which asking this question (or the possibility of asking this question) is a feature of our engagement. For example, we are attuned to journalists overreaching themselves. If a journalist claims that, for example, 'there is panic in the cabinet over this issue' we can rightly ask whether (or how) they know this. This is not restricted to straightforward documentary narratives, however. We are also sensitive to such claims in hypothetical narratives, where the point is to instruct. We might wonder at the credentials of someone who confidently asserts that, were a wolf to run into the cave, it would run to the left. When we are less concerned to form beliefs on the basis of engaging with the narrative, the issue of the epistemological credentials of the narrative agency becomes less salient. If a reader believes, of the narrative in front of them, that someone has made it up in order to entertain, the question of 'how does the narrator know...' will not arise.

Impossible Fictions

Some fictional narratives appear to describe states of affairs that are logically impossible; a particularly blatant case might be one in which 2+2 did not equal 4 (Gendler 2000). This generates a prima facie problem for the standard account of our engaging with fiction.

1. In engaging with a fiction, we imagine its content.
2. The content of some fictions is logically impossible.
3. We cannot imagine the logically impossible.

The conventional view does not entail (1), although holders of the view generally endorse it. The view only entails one ought to imagine that content of the fiction in order to get a 'full appreciation' of the work (Walton 2006: 145).[3] I also—obviously—reject (1), and need to show that an analogous problem does not arise. For me, the question would be the compatibility of the following three claims.

1*. We engage with representations.
2*. The content of some fictions is logically impossible.
3*. We cannot engage with the logically impossible.

Before I show that this is not a problem for my view (there is no reason to believe 3*) I will enter a caveat, make a remark about (2), and show why (3*) is false.

The caveat is that there is a problem here for those who are interested in providing a semantics for fiction. One might, for example, follow David Lewis and attempt to provide the truth conditions for F(p) modelled on the semantics for modal discourse in terms of possible worlds (Lewis 1978).[4] Possible worlds cannot, however, model logical impossibility which raises the problem of either doing running repairs on the Lewisian project or finding a different semantics altogether. I am unsure of the relation between the semantic project and the project of this book (let us call that 'the phenomenological project'); at times, they seem to be pursued independently. My view—although I am not sure I could defend it against determined opposition—is that the phenomenological project has priority. If it turns out (as I will argue it does) that the division between impossible and possible fictions is largely irrelevant to our experience of fiction, it leaves me wondering what the semantic project—for which this does seem the crucial distinction—is about. Both projects are still grasping towards clarity, and it might be that when each achieves enlightenment, they will be able to illuminate each other.

Having entered that caveat, let me move on to commenting on (2). Consider the following three cases.[5]

---

[3] Kathleen Stock also holds that what is fictional need not be imaginable (Stock 2003: 108).
[4] Gregory Currie has provided reasons for being sceptical of the success of this project (Currie 1990: 74–5). Craig Bourne and Emily Caddick Bourne defend a Lewisian position in (Bourne and Caddick Bourne 2016).
[5] The existence of cases such as these casts strong doubt on the relevance to understanding fiction of attempts to provide psychological underpinnings for failure to imagine impossibility (Nichols 2006; Weinberg and Meskin 2006).

In the first Superman movie, Lois Lane dies when her car is buried by earth. Superman then flies around the earth in the reverse direction to that in which it is spinning. This causes the direction of the spin of the earth to reverse, which causes time to run backwards, which brings us to a point before Lois is killed, and she can therefore be saved.

In *The Wind in the Willows*, in which animals such as moles, water rats, and toads wear clothes and talk to each other, Ratty's picnic basket contains cold chicken, cold tongue, cold ham, cold beef, and various potted meats (Grahame 1971: 14).

The following occurs in *Alice Through the Looking-Glass*:

'Crawling at your feet' said the Gnat (Alice drew her feet back in some alarm), 'you may observe a Bread-and-butter-fly. Its wings are think slices of bread-and-butter, its body is a crust, and its head is a lump of sugar.'
    'And what does *it* live on?'
    'Weak tea with cream in it.' (Carroll 2010: 27)

Philosophers are sophisticated about possibility in at least two ways. First, they identify different kinds of possibility: physical possibility, logical possibility, and metaphysical possibility being the three most prominent. Second, they are sophisticated about what is or is not possible; for example, philosophers generally disagree with the folk view that travelling back in time is possible. Most philosophers (I would guess) would regard all of the quotations above as describing logically impossible states of affairs. Quite apart from the bizarre causation, Superman (as I have just said) could not travel back in time. In the other two cases, one does not have to be too essentialist to think that anything that has the properties possessed by the characters in question is incompatible with their stated species classification. That is, anything that wears goggles, cap, gaiters, and an enormous overcoat, speaks English, owns a stately home and is prone to passing fits of enthusiasm about vehicular transport is not a toad, and yet Toad clearly is a toad.

However, given that there is disagreement within philosophy about possibility (not all philosophers agree on the impossibility of travel back in time, and not all philosophers are essentialists, and, if they are, are not all essentialists of the same stripe) there will be no unanimity on whether or not the state of affairs is impossible. The claim that the impossibility of a narrative will bother the ordinary reader presupposes that they are able to perform two demanding tasks. First, they need to have the resources to get a clear and distinct grasp of what is being described (as we have seen, Walton and Stock deny this is necessary for what is being described being fictional). Second, they need to be able to work out whether or not what is being described is possible. I doubt they have the resources to perform either task. That is, I doubt whether the average viewer of *Superman I*, or reader of *The Wind in the Willows*, or *Alice Through the Looking Glass* would know whether or not they were possible. Unless the contradiction is blatant—and contrary to the background principles established by the narrative—they are unlikely to notice.

In Chapter 5 and 6 I discussed the psychology of text processing, and concluded that even on a relatively rich construal readers form a fairly minimal mental model of the overall state of affairs described in a text. The basis for (3) is that we cannot imagine logically impossible states of affairs. This view is controversial. If it is to stand any chance of being true, what must be impossible is that we can imagine the state of affairs in depth. That is, what is at issue is 'ideal conceivability': conceivability based on 'ideal rational reflection' (Chalmers 2002). The key point, which is enough to show (3*) to be false, is that there is no evidence that readers do, in the course of reading a narrative, indulge in anything like such ideal conceivability. According to the models of text processing I discussed, readers track local coherence, or local and global coherence, depending on their strategy. If the reader notices an incoherence it takes them longer to process the text (indeed, this is how we know that they have noticed the incoherence).

Faced with an incoherence a reader can do one of four things. He or she could take the story to be a misreport; that is, take the narrator to be mistaken or lying. If this were the case the reader would reject the claim as false; both false in the narrative and, if the events were being reported as actual, false per se (I shall call this 'the rejection strategy'). The reader could think hard and find a way in which the narrative could be made coherent (I shall call this 'the reconciliation strategy'). The reader could reclassify the narrative; that is, attribute to the world it describes a principle in which the situation is no longer contradictory (I shall call this the 'weird world strategy'). Finally, the reader could simply ignore that part of the narrative or put it aside as a flaw, and try to make sense of the rest without it (I shall call this the 'disregarding strategy').

Let us take the story of Lazarus' resurrection as our example of a narrative. I shall assume that this is, prima facie, a report of events that occurred in the actual world. According to the reality principle, if an organism is dead then the organism stays dead. According to the narrative, Lazarus was an organism, Lazarus was dead, and yet Lazarus did not stay dead. If the reader adopted the rejection strategy he or she would reject either the claim that Lazarus was dead or the claim that he did not stay dead as false; false in the narrative and false in the actual world. If the reader adopted the reconciliation strategy, he or she will conclude (say) that Lazarus had never really been dead; rather he was in some coma that gave all the appearances of being dead. The weird world strategy would lead the reader to cease thinking of the story as describing the actual world, but rather a world that does not obey the reality principle. The disregarding strategy is more difficult in this case; if the reader either ignores or excises the contradiction, there will not be much left of the narrative.

Let us consider each strategy in slightly greater depth. The rejection and reconciliation strategies are the two options if the reader has independent reason to believe that the narrative obeys the reality principle—in particular, if the reader believes the narrative is non-fictional. If he or she adopts the rejection strategy, the reader will take the narrator to be deliberately lying or to be in some way or other unreliable. The upshot is that the reader does not hold the incoherent claim to be true in the narrative (and in cases of non-fiction he or she does not hold it to be true of the world). The reconciliation strategy attempts to find a way, within the realms of reality, in which the story could be true. This is the option taken by those desperate attempts to provide naturalistic explanations of Biblical miracles. It is not essential that the narratives be non-fictional; the same two strategies can be used to deal with apparent incoherences in fictional narratives that obey the reality principle. Late in Emily Bronte's *Wuthering Heights*, which has established itself in the reader's mind as a novel that obeys the reality principle, Heathcliff opens the grave of Catherine, who has been dead for eighteen years. Her face is undecayed ('I saw her face again—it is hers yet!' (Bronte 1963: 246)). The reader detects a global incoherence: on the one hand, a body that has been in the grave for eighteen years should have decayed and on the other the body is not decayed. If the reader adopts the rejection strategy he or she will reject that claim that her face was undecayed as part of the narrative. He or she might claim instead that, in a moment of extreme emotional turmoil, Heathcliff misreported the state of Catherine's face. Alternatively, the reader might attempt the reconciliation strategy and try to make the apparently conflicting claims coherent—perhaps by speculating that Catherine was buried in lime that prevented decay.

For narratives that are believed not to obey the reality principle, at least attempting the weird world strategy is all but inevitable. If a reader adopts this strategy, then, when faced with an event that looks incoherent the reader takes the report of the event to be accurate and revises his or her principles of generation. That is, they allow that Lazarus did not stay dead, and revise the principles of generation to allow the dead not to stay dead (it is that sort of world). There are certain narratives where it is simply unclear whether the reader should stick with the reality principle, and try to work with the rejection, reconciliation, or disregarding strategies, or use the weird world strategy. *Wuthering Heights* is a classic case; should the reader stick with it being a realist novel, or alter their view of the principles of generation—treating the novel as part of the Gothic genre which allows deviations from the reality principle? Sometimes this is done with considerable verve. In Chapter 6 I gave the example of *Master and Margarita*, a novel in which the reader's ability to stick with the reality principle matches the characters' difficulty to explain events using orthodox Marxist materialism. Other cases are aesthetically less worthy; these are cases in which there is no consistency to the principles of generation. In such cases the reader is invited to adopt an 'anything goes' strategy. What kind of world could it be in which people are massively technologically advanced and fight with swords? In which a person is invulnerable to the slings and arrows of life's misfortune but is in danger? [6] In such cases, the disregarding strategy beckons.

The disregarding strategy can apply either to the events or to the principles of generation. An example of the first would be sensible strategy to apply to the absence of decay of Cathy's face in *Wuthering Heights*. That is, disregard it as a regrettable anomaly (although the reasons for the anomaly might themselves be interesting) and maintain the reality principle as the principle of generation. However, it is more usual to apply the strategy to the principles of generation themselves. Readers encode that the world is one in which Superman can do the things he does, that rats and moles can converse and live in houses, and that insects can be made of bread

---

[6] '…fantasy not directed to the past has now shifted from exotic peoples to extraterrestrials. Since they can offer no concrete resistance at all to the most primitive fantasies, the results are pathetically or repulsively impoverished' (Williams 1985: 220).

and butter and live on tea, without thinking too much about it. The incoherences are never salient as they are lost in the general looseness of the
mental model. With all but the worst works, the principles do not lose all
their power to guide what is or is not incoherent. The world of *Superman*
is not one in which Superman can, without reason, lose his vulnerability
to Kryptonite; the world of *Wind in the Willows* is not one in which Ratty
can dine on Mole (as he can dine on pigs and chickens); and the world of
Alice Through the Looking-Glass is not one in which Alice can suddenly
call down help from aliens.[7]

Authors who rely on the disregarding strategy can sometimes fail.
Whether they do so is partly a matter of the temperament of the reader.
The same incoherence might be 'disregardable' for some and not for others. Consider the case of someone (let us call him or her 'the philosopher')
watching *Eternal Sunshine of a Spotless Mind*, a film in which large chunks
of people's memories are erased without the effects ramifying. The philosopher finds this simply incoherent: memory is not so modular. Furthermore,
there is no satisfactory principle of generation: this is a narrative in which
the reality principle is intended to hold for people's psychologies *apart from
this fact*. The philosopher might try to disregard this, but find it difficult to
enter into the exploration of the subtleties of human psychologies that are
completely incoherent. It might irritate him or her that the fictional world is
not workable, and no effort was put in to make it workable.[8] *Stranger Than
Fiction*, in which a tax inspector discovers he is in fact a fictional character
in a partly-written novel, is also not workable. However, the disregarding
strategy might work for the philosopher. The film wears its unworkability
on its sleeve; it is as if it asks us to note and then ignore the incoherence, so
as to benefit from undoubted virtues of the patently daft plot.

In short, readers have a number of strategies for dealing with perceived
incoherence in a narrative (and, recall, there might be incoherence that
readers do not perceive). The relevant distinction—at least for the phenomenological project—is not between possible and impossible narratives, but between narratives that obey the reality principle and narratives
that do not, and then, within the latter group, narratives where one or
more of the strategies work and narratives in which they do not. In short,

---

[7] On this point, it is salutary to consider the extreme weirdness of the last book of Mervyn
Peake's *Gormenghast* trilogy.

[8] I should record John Holbo's valiant effort to convince me I am completely wrong about
this film.

the relevant distinction is between straightforward and weird narratives, and within weird narratives, ones that work and ones that do not work.

All that I have said is compatible with the truth of (3); that we cannot imagine (in the sense of 'ideally rationally conceive') the logically impossible. Indeed, one cannot come to a 'full appreciation' of many fictions. To take just one of the examples above, the world of *Wind in the Willows* is distinctly odd and if one thinks about it too much it dissolves. Rats, moles, and toads wear clothes and converse, but eat other animals. The relationship between Toad (a toad) and the washerwoman's daughter (a human being) flounders because of class differences. It is impossible to form a full understanding of a world in which these and other states of affairs are unremarkable. The disregarding strategy beckons; we simply lose all this incoherence in the looseness of the mental model.

The 'Fictionality Puzzle'

The previous section discussed impossible narratives. In a brief discussion in *Mimesis as Make-Believe*, Kendall Walton introduces an intriguing issue that looks similar to the above, but really is quite different. Walton points out that there seem to be limits on what propositions can be true-in-a-fiction.

> We must be prepared to assume it to be fictional that bloodletting cures disease, that the sun revolves around the earth, that people think with their hearts...but not that the only good Indian is a dead one or that slavery is just and torture in the service of tyranny humane. (Walton 1990: 154)

The subsequent history of the problem has been philosophically fairly disastrous. In an interesting and influential paper published in 2000 Tamar Gendler coined the catchy moniker 'the puzzle of imaginative resistance' (Gendler 2000). However, the catchiness was not an aid to clarity as it is not clear that the problem on which Walton focused in 1990 has anything to do with either the imagination or resistance. Gendler has subsequently written that use of the expression 'imaginative resistance' is 'imprudent' (Gendler 2006: 150), and Walton has written, rather ruefully, that, of the phrase 'the puzzle of imaginative resistance' the only word about which he has no complaints is 'of' (Walton 2006: 146).[9]

---

[9] Vexingly, it turns out 'the fictionality puzzle' is also a misnomer. As I will show below, the problem arises for all representations, not only fictional representations.

Given the number of different discussions that flourish in this particular hedgerow it is as well to be precise as to the one in which I am interested: it is the problem Brian Weatherson calls 'the alethic puzzle' and Walton calls 'the fictionality puzzle' (Weatherson 2004; Walton 2006: 138).[10] The problem can be stated quite simply. For some proposition p and some narrative N (where N can be non-fictional or fictional):

A. P is true-in-N if p is asserted in N.

(A) can fail in at least four ways.[11] First, it might be that p is asserted in N but that the actual author has slipped up. Second, it might be that p is asserted in N but that the narrator is unreliable, that the narrator later changes their mind about p, or that p is asserted ironically, sarcastically and so on. I shall refer to these both under the heading 'determinacy failure'. Second, the narrative might for other reasons be locally and globally incoherent such that understanding it is either impossible, or, if not impossible, simply not worth the effort. I shall call this 'coherence failure'. Third, it fails for certain types of proposition. Above, Walton gives us one of these: some propositions that express a moral falsehood. He has also discussed a number of others including cases in which p falsely claims a joke is funny or p claims that something trivial (the example is nutmeg) is the *summum bonum*. I shall call this 'transmission failure'. Determinacy failure and coherence failure are philosophically unproblematic; it is transmission failure that characterizes the fictionality puzzle.

The Sherlock Holmes stories provide a famous example of the first way N can fail because of an error on behalf of the actual author. Watson's war wound (assuming there was just the one) is given two locations. In *A Study in Scarlet* its location is given as his shoulder and in *The Sign of Four* he sits nursing 'a wounded leg'. Given the existence of the other, neither assertion makes the proposition asserted true-in-the-narrative.

---

[10] My neglect of the other discussions is not entirely because of considerations of space; I concur with Walton's view that, for at least most of them, it is difficult to see why they are either puzzling or interesting (Walton 2006).

[11] The qualification is because I cannot rule out, *a priori*, that there might not be other ways, or that my first, second, and third way may not be further sub-divided. Nonetheless, the fourth way presents the interesting problem, and I am not sure that sub-dividing the first three ways further would be worthwhile.

The second way N can fail can be illustrated by a passage from Ring Lardner's novel, *You Know Me Al*. This consists of a series of letters written by a baseball pitcher home to his friend Al. The narrator ('the busher') portrays himself as generous, brave, and a success with women. It is true-in-the-narrative that he is mean, cowardly, and utterly blind as to the machinations of the opposite sex. Consider the following passage:

Now I can make Violet my wife and she's got Hazel beat forty ways. She ain't nowheres near as big as Hazel but she's classier Al and she will make me a good wife. She ain't never asked me for no money. (Lardner 1946: 71)

Within this narrative, the following proposition is asserted.

q: Violet has never asked the busher for any money.

As I have said, the narrative makes it evident that the busher is self-deluded and a case study in confirmation bias. That is, the reader has grounds for thinking that the narrator is unreliable: he reports others' comments about him whose meaning is opaque to him but transparent to the reader; he rules out certain actions in one letter, only to do them by the next; he transparently ignores any evidence that does not confirm his self-image; and so and so forth. The author has represented the narrator as someone who does not know what is going on; someone who is epistemically incompetent. This is an example of determinacy failure because the fictional narrator lacks self-knowledge. Determinacy failure because of irony or sarcasm is frequently met in political speeches, both non-fictional and fictional. It is not true-in-the-narrative that Brutus is an honourable man no matter how often Mark Anthony makes that assertion. The reader should adopt the rejection strategy detailed in the last section and conclude that q is not true-in-the-narrative. In both these cases (that of Holmes and that of the busher) (A) fails because of determinacy failure. In cases of determinacy failure it makes sense for the reader to adopt the rejection strategy: the asserted claim is not true in the narrative.

I argued in the last section that local and global incoherence in the narrative can make it either impossible to understand or undermine the reader's will to understand it. This is coherence failure, and it can also lead to a failure of (A). In a paper that is otherwise admirable for its taxonomy, Brian Weatherson is guilty of confusing coherence failure with transmission failure. To see what distinguishes the two let us consider one of Weatherson's examples (originally from Yablo 2002: 485).

They flopped down beneath the giant maple. One more item to find, and yet the game seemed lost. Hang on, Sally said. It's staring us in the face. This is a *maple* tree we're under. She grabbed a five-fingered leaf. Here was the oval they needed! They ran off to claim their prize. (Weatherson 2004: 4)

As I have said, faced with incoherence readers can adopt the reconciliation, weird world, or disregarding strategy. The weird world strategy is all but inevitable in non-realist narratives; readers go back and forth between bothersome incoherence and formulating a principle of generation for that narrative that replaces incoherence by coherence. In this narrative, such as it is, the opportunities are limited. The reader is faced with a bothersome incoherence: there is an object which has the property of being a five-fingered leaf and the property of being an oval. Are they able to generate a principle of generation which will both accommodate this and allow them to build a mental model of the world of the story? Perhaps it could be done, but why bother? The effort expended would clearly outweigh the reward gained. The disregarding strategy is similarly unappealing as, if we disregard the incoherence of an object which has the property of being a five-fingered leaf and the property of being an oval, there will not be much of the story left. In short, what characterizes coherence failure is that the reader is unable or unwilling to generate a workable principle of generation so the process of understanding the text grinds to a halt. Most (but not all) of Weatherson's examples can be explained in the same way.[12]

Determinacy failure and coherence failure do not raise interesting philosophical issues. The case is different, however, when we consider transmission failure. In his (non-fictional) account of his travels in the Amazon, *Brazilian Adventure*, Peter Fleming tells of the experience of being part of an ill-fated mission into the rainforest to find the remains of Colonel Fawcett. He recounts how he and his colleague, Bob, are abandoned by the bulk of the expedition and left to an uncertain future. As they turn back towards civilization, the following incident occurs:

As we strapped on our still sodden loads an enormous alligator, the biggest I have ever seen, came quietly gliding up the narrow channel opposite our camp . . . here was a chance to work off some of our resentment against unkind circumstances; and as it drew level I took a careful shot with the .22 and got it in the eye.

---

[12] 'Alien Robbery', 'Cats and Dogs', 'Wiggins World', 'A Quixotic Victory', and 'Fixing a Hole' are instances of coherence failure. 'Death on a Freeway' and (to an extent) 'The Benefactor' are instances of transmission failure.

It was probably the most phenomenal result ever produced with a rook rifle. The peaceful river boiled. The alligator thrashed its head from side to side in agony. Then, as the tiny bullet touched (I suppose) its brain, it reared itself out upon the further bank and lay there, killed with a crumb of lead. (Fleming 1964: 251)

Certain things are true in this narrative: that Fleming discharged a rifle and that he killed an alligator. The text also conveys something else: that shooting the alligator was an appropriate way for him to ease his frustrations. The puzzle is that although this is asserted or implied in the narrative, it is not true in the narrative (I am assuming that the wilful destruction of a complicated organism simply to ease one's frustrations is morally unacceptable). Much ink has been expended on whether the reader *cannot* accept this as true in the narrative or is *unwilling* to accept this as true in the narrative (Gendler 2006). This strikes me as a mistake. That these propositions are not true in the narrative is not something that can be sorted out after the fact, as it were; it needs to be built into the structure of our understanding narratives. That is, it should be sorted out as part of the process of our engaging with narratives.

What our example shows is that the answer is relatively simple. Provided there is no determinacy failure, if Fleming asserts in the narrative (that is, he testifies) that he discharged his rifle and killed an alligator, than it is true in the narrative that Fleming discharged his rifle and killed an alligator. However, the question of whether it was appropriate to kill an alligator simply to ease his frustration is not up to Fleming: it is up to the reader. Notice, the asymmetry applies even for claims with which the reader agrees. Consider the following passage from the same book.

The only person who had a bad time during this stage of our journey was Bob, who went down with fever on the second day out of Conceição. We gave him quinine and hoped for the best. Considering the conditions under which we were living, he bore up remarkably well. He had to lie all day in the bottom of the boat... with no shelter from the sun except the stifling awning of a blanket. At night we carried him ashore and dumped him on the camp-bed with which he alone—providentially sybaritic—had burdened the expedition; and then, if we were travelling by night, we picked him up a few hours later and dumped him in the boat again. (Fleming 1964: 313)

It is true in the narrative that one ought to aid one's colleague who is unwell. We need to distinguish ways in which a proposition being true or false in the narrative can be grounded. The first is (A). An example from our first passage would be that Fleming killed an alligator and an example from our second passage would be that Fleming carried his colleague. The second is judgements we bring to the narrative on the basis of its content, whether or not the contents of those judgements are asserted in the narrative. It is the latter that are candidates for transmission failure.

Consider a third example: a speaker is describing the activities of the local council and points out that the vegetarian option has been withdrawn from free meals for the elderly. The morality of this is not made true in the speech by (A); whether or not this is a good development is up to the listeners. Let us divide the listeners into 'naysayers' (those who think the elderly should be offered the choice) and 'yeasayers' (those who are either indifferent or opposed to the elderly being offered the choice). If the speaker goes on to assert that the council's decision is morally sound that is not the ground for either naysayers or yeasayers thinking the moral soundness of the decision is true in the speech. The speaker cannot rely on (A) to make the moral soundness of the council's decision true in the speech. The same would be true if the speaker (or Fleming) had claimed that nutmeg is the *summum bonum* or that some dreadful 'knock knock' joke was funny. The limits of the kinds of propositions can be true because of (A) are the limits of the kinds of information we are willing to accept on the authority of others.[13]

Transmission failure is related to the failure of moral testimony (although narratives are not typically trying to convince us of moral claims, rather they are simply laying moral claims before us as true or false). The paradigm case of testimony is where person A believes some proposition on the say-so of person B, where person B is in a better position to know than person A. I do not have to take a position on whether moral testimony is possible, and, if it is possible, what exactly is conveyed (although, as we shall see below, this disavowal returns to haunt me). For my purposes, it matters only that moral testimony is recognized as problematic. If there are circumstances in which moral testimony (of whatever sort) is possible, then it will apply to narratives. In other words, my position faces a happy dilemma. In circumstances (if any) in which testimony is legitimate transmission failure will not occur and there is no question to be answered. In circumstances in which testimony is not

---

[13] Kathleen Stock has written, of my earlier account, that there is a gap in my argument here in that the grounds for doubting the speaker (narrator) have not been given (Stock. 2005.: 613). I cannot grasp her worry, but perhaps this reformulation might alleviate it.

legitimate, transmission failure will occur and be explained by the failure of testimony.

In an earlier version of this account, I put the point by claiming that we have independent reason for thinking that engaging with a fictional narrative is modelled on engaging with a non-fictional narrative. The example I used was a report from a foreign correspondent. In non-fictional narrative the narrator (the correspondent) is in a privileged epistemological position on certain issues (roughly, the facts of the matter) and not on other issues (the kinds of propositions for which transmission failure occurs). The solution to the fictionality problem follows: we accept the former kinds of proposition and not the latter (Matravers 2003). Brian Weatherson has criticized this approach.

The problem with this approach is that there are several salient disanalogies between the position of the correspondent and that of the fictional narrator. The following case, which I heard about from Mark Liberman, illustrates this nicely. On March 5, 2004, the BBC reported that children in a nursery in England had found a frog with three heads and six legs. Many people, including Professor Liberman, were sceptical, notwithstanding the fact that the BBC was actually in England and Professor Liberman was not. The epistemological privilege generated by proximity doesn't extend to implausible claims about three-headed frogs. The obvious disanalogy is that if a fictional narrator said that there was a three-headed six-legged frog in the children's nursery, then other things being equal, we would infer it is true in the fiction that there was indeed a three-headed six-legged frog in the children's nursery. So there isn't an easy analogy between when we trust foreign correspondents and when we trust fictional narrators. Now we need an explanation of why the analogy does hold when either party makes morally deviant claims, even though it doesn't when they both make biologically deviant claims. But it doesn't seem any easier to say why the analogy holds then than it is to solve the original puzzle. (Weatherson 2004: 11)

There is a simple explanation of why the analogy holds in the case of morally deviant claims but not in the case of biologically deviant claims. It does not hold in the case of biologically deviant claims because such claims are cases of determinacy failure. The narrative from the BBC, being about the actual world, obeys the reality principle. The claim that there is a frog with three heads and six legs does not cohere with our beliefs about reality. Hence, we need to adopt either the rejection or reconciliation strategy. The BBC is generally reliable, but it can err. Is it more likely that there was a three-headed six-legged frog as they report or that a mistake has been made? Like Professor Liberman I would be inclined to think a mistake has been made and adopt the rejection strategy. That is, the claim is not true in the narrative. It is worth reiterating the point made above (the example used was *Wuthering Heights*) that the same strategy can be employed for claims that do not cohere with reality in fictions that adhere to the reality principle. In Fred Vargas' novel *Have Mercy on Us All* one of the characters, Joss, finds himself in a bar: 'Joss stared vacantly at the stately silhouette of his great-great-grandfather as he slipped off his bar stool with considerable style.' Here the reconciliation strategy is appropriate: we reject the claim as being true in the narrative, instead replacing it with something compatible with reality, such as 'Joss visualized his great-great-grandfather slipping off his bar stool with considerable style.' Of course, as Weatherson points out, if the narrative does not obey the reality principle (for example, in tales told in the children's nursery) then the weird world strategy is appropriate and the claims will almost certainly come out as being true in the narrative. We cannot tell a similar story for narratives—any narratives—that make morally deviant claims because such claims are subject to transmission failure: (A) is not a way of making such claims true in the narrative.

There is, however, one issue that threatens to undermine the view; I shall call it 'the revenge fictionality puzzle'.[14] Let us return to the excerpt from Peter Fleming, and refer to the claim that it is morally acceptable to destroy a complicated organism simply to ease one's frustrations as 'r'. On my view the structure of fictionality failure is as follows:

1. The narrative contains r.
2. Transmission failure means that (A) is not a means of making r true in the narrative.
3. If a reader thinks r is false, he or she will think r is false in the narrative.

One way of stating the revenge fictionality puzzle (which I will argue in a moment is misleading) is to point out that Fleming's is an actual-world narrative, to which actual world morality applies. The fictionality puzzle asks why (3) should apply to fictions. My solution works only if the reader of a fiction engages with a representation of non-actual events using their actual moral beliefs. However, this discounts a possibility. Why can they

---

[14]   Both Rob Hopkins and Kendall Walton have pointed this out to me.

not assume a non-actual persona (one who does not find the claims made in the narrative morally problematic) and get on with enjoying whatever fiction it is that they are reading?

The revenge fictionality puzzle arises naturally on Walton's view. Walton 'is inclined to think' that imagining is essentially self-referential; that is, imagining that p involves 'imagining oneself believing or knowing it' (Walton 1990: 28, 215). Thus, for Walton, readers of fiction are reflexive props: they imagine of themselves that they believe the content of the fiction. They are participants in the game of make-believe. As it is part of the theory that they are playing themselves, room opens up to ask why their fictional selves have the moral dispositions of their actual selves. They imagine they have beliefs that they do not have so what is to prevent them imagining they have moral beliefs they do not have?

My view does not have *these* reasons for the revenge fictionality puzzle as, on my view, there is no difference between engaging with a non-fictional and fictional narrative (what difference there is, is manifested in the relation of the content of the narrative to pre-existing structures of belief). This does not free me from the problem, however; it simply makes things worse. On my view, the fictionality puzzle simply arises for *all* representations[15]: what prevents a reader—whether of Peter Fleming or his novelist brother Ian—from adopting a different set of moral beliefs if not doing so prevents them from engaging with a narrative? To reiterate: it will not do to pose the question as follows: the reader countenances as true-in-the-narrative all manner of states of affairs he or she believes false or even impossible, so why can they not countenance certain false moral claims as being true-in-the-narrative? We already have an answer to that: because they are not the kinds of claim that *can* be made true-in-a-narrative on the grounds of (A). We need to put the question directly: why do readers not imagine, of themselves, that they have different moral views?

Note that a reader *can* at least attempt this. A method actor playing a white supremacist might check whether they are successfully inhabiting their role by reading *The Turner Diaries* (a white supremacist novel) or *Mein Kampf* and seeing what they make of the narrative's content. Nonetheless, why do readers not do this? That is, why is it not part of the

---

[15] Hence, the misnomer. Of course, it is only a misnomer if by 'fiction' we mean 'fiction as traditionally conceived'. If by 'fiction' Walton means—as I have suggested he ought—*all* representations, there he, at least, is not in error.

reader's standard repertoire? The proposal is that readers provisionally adopt a moral principle, alien to their actual selves, so that their moral judgements can simply go along with those expressed in the narrative.

I do not know the answer to this question, but suspect the reasons lie in the direction of the reasons for the failure of moral testimony.[16] Robert Hopkins and Alison Hills have been developing a thought that looks promising. Hopkins points out that moral testimony could fail for one of two reasons. First, that testimony makes knowledge *unavailable* to the recipient and, second, that it makes the knowledge *unusable* by the recipient for some further reason. He argues that the second is more plausible and 'there is some further norm proscribing adopting one's moral beliefs on the word of others'. His suggestion for such a norm is as follows.

The Requirement: having the right to a moral belief requires one to grasp the *moral* grounds for it. (Hopkins 2007: 630)

This is close to Hill's suggestion that being able to use a moral belief requires more than moral knowledge (which testimony might give) but moral understanding.

If you understand why X is morally right or wrong, you must have some appreciation of the reasons why it is wrong. Appreciating the reasons why it is wrong is not the same as simply believing that they are the reasons why it is wrong, or even knowing that they are the reasons why it is wrong. Moral understanding involves a grasp of the relation between a moral proposition and the reasons why it is true.

You cannot really understand why *p* is true if *p* and the reasons why *p* are the only things about the subject of which you are aware: it is not possible to understand why some isolated fact is true. If you have this kind of appreciation of moral reasons, you must have, at least to some extent, a systematic grasp of morality. This is not, of course, to say that you need to have a grasp of anything that could possibly be morally important. (Hills 2009: 101)

The thought is this. A reader can attempt to 'take on' an alien moral view; we have already seen that. However, in morality there is a norm that one cannot operate with a moral view unless one has a grasp of its moral grounds (in Hopkins' terminology) or one understands it (in Hill's terminology). We cannot understand how something could be a moral reason

---

[16]   As stated above, Kathleen Stock thinks general failure of moral testimony insufficient to ground an explanation of fictionality failure, and instead appeals to a failure of understanding. It might be that she is asking for an account of failure of moral testimony. If so, I am following her solution.

for the denigration of non-white ethnic groups or the mass extermination of Jews.

In his 1994 paper, Walton speculated that what lies at the bottom of the fictionality puzzle is 'something to do with an inability to imagine [the relevant kind of supervenience relations] being different from how we think they are' (Walton 1994: 46). He endorses this in his 2006 paper, although stresses that it is compatible with our imagining the impossible and also with the impossible being fictional. What seems to be important 'is a very particular kind of imaginative inability, one that attaches to propositions expressing certain sorts of supervenience relations, which the imaginer rejects' (Walton 2006: 146). Although Walton clearly wants to restrict his speculation to fictions, the reason seems to me to be general and to be part of the explanation of transmission failure—which applies to both non-fictional and fictional narratives.

10

Coda: Film

Hitherto, most of my discussion has been limited to our engagement with the written word. However, much of what I have said applies also to our interaction with film, and the contemporary literature on film (I shall, once again, restrict myself to the literature in the Anglo-American tradition) exhibits many of the same confusions identified earlier. I shall revert to my previous terminology and refer to the claim that the imagination is required to distinguish between fiction and non-fiction films as 'the consensus view'. Many of the arguments against applying the consensus view to film are identical to the arguments against applying the consensus view to literature. The argument we met in Chapter 3 that attempted to argue for the existence of a mental state peculiar to fiction from absence of motivation was in terms of cinema audiences. We saw there that absence of motivation was fully explained by the fact that the audiences believed they were in a representation relation, and was nothing to do with whether the representation was fictional or non-fictional. I have argued that what undermines the consensus view is that it attempts to distinguish fictional propositions from non-fictional propositions by maintaining that we are mandated to imagine the former and believe the latter. However, according to the account of the imagination that is provided, we are mandated to imagine the contents of all representations whether they are non-fictional or fictional. We find evidence of the consensus view all over the literature. Here, for example, it is in the work of Gregory Currie. He contrasts those features of a film which are factual with those that are non-factual, claiming belief is the appropriate attitude for the first and imagination for the second (his example is *All the President's Men*).

Woodward is depicted as having a certain appearance, namely that of Robert Redford. Redford, Hoffman and the other actors speak certain words and speak them in certain ways in certain settings, all this plainly visible on screen. None of this is intended to be attributed to Woodward and Bernstein. These are fictional things; we are to imagine them happening, we are not intended to believe they happened. (Currie 1999: 150–1)

I shall not rehearse the problems entailed by the attempt to use the imagination for this purpose.

I shall consider a use of the imagination distinctive to the philosophy of film: namely, that the imagination is required to describe the relation between the audience and what happens on the screen. To do that, I need first to say something about the role of the imagination in depictive representations. The claim that imagination is required in order to experience something as a depictive representation is associated with Kendall Walton. Walton argues that a depiction 'is a representation whose function is to serve as a prop in reasonably rich and vivid perceptual games of make-believe' (Walton 1990: 296). Walton gives his theory in terms of a painting (Hobbema's *Wooded Landscape with a Water Mill*) although it is clear from his examples that this generalizes to film. Here is the account in more detail:

Rather than merely imagining seeing a mill, as a result of actually seeing the canvas (as one may imagine seeing Emma upon reading a description of her appearance in *Madame Bovary*), one imagines one's seeing of the canvas to be a seeing of a mill, and this imagining is an integral part of one's visual experience of the canvas. (Walton 1990: 301. See also Walton 1992)

As we saw in Chapter 2, this analysis combined with the claim that anything that serves as a prop in a game of make-believe is a fiction commits Walton to the view that 'pictures are fiction by definition' (Walton 1990: 351).

I will illustrate the problem Walton is attempting to solve, the nature of depiction, with an example drawn from film (and I shall focus on film from here on). The experience of seeing a film of a young woman playing a piano is distinct from the experience of seeing a young woman playing in one's immediate visual environment. This raises the philosophical question of the light we can throw on the former experience: what is it to see an image of a young woman playing a piano and what relation does this bear to the equivalent face-to-face experience? This problem has attracted a formidable literature (for a snapshot of the current debate, see Abell and Bantinaki, 2010) to which I will not add. The argument in this chapter is a conditional one: if imagination is not involved in engaging with depictive representations in virtue of the analysis of depiction what role (if any) does it have? In other words (ignoring the possibility of other analyses in terms of imagination) if Walton is wrong about depiction is there any role for the imagination in our engaging with still or moving pictures?

To lend a little more substance to the dialectic I attempt to explain what inclines me against Walton's view. His view could be interpreted as an answer to one of two questions. The first is a causal question: by what mechanism are we caused to have our visual experience of film? The second is a constitutive question: given that looking at a film is not like looking at the events depicted face-to-face, what is the most perspicuous description of looking at a film?

In answer to the first, causal, question it would be the view that an exercise of the imagination *results* in a rich and vivid game of make-believe. One may doubt whether such an explanation would work—Why would our imagining effect such a transformation of our phenomenology?—but that need not matter here. What interests me is the nature of the experience of engagement and whether the visual experience is best thought of as an imaginative experience. There is independent reason to think that Walton was not aiming to answer the first question. That is, he takes his account to be an elucidation of Richard Wollheim's notion of 'seeing in', and Wollheim is best interpreted as providing an answer to the second question (Walton 1992). Whatever the intention, I shall take Walton to be answering the second question. The issue, then, is whether we need to invoke the imagination to provide a constitutive account of the nature of the experience of film.

My scepticism springs from the simple thought that I cannot grasp how the perception of an image can be an act of imagination. It would be a decisive point in Walton's favour if an imaginative project somehow featured consciously in our experience—however, that is no part of his claim (Walton 1992: 285). When watching a film, we observe images of events. It hardly seems worth backing this point up with empirical evidence, but results suggest that recall of the content of visual representations have more in common with perceptions (they have 'more sensory and contextual information') than recall of the contents of representations that have merely presented to us verbally (Johnson 1988: 390). Malcolm Budd has pointed out the various ways in which the experience of a visual image has prima facie properties that are at odds with it being imagined.

So if our imagination plays the role assigned to it by Walton in the perception of pictures it needs to be capable of more or less instantaneous, highly stable, and detailed content, triggered to imagine just the same objects of vision on looking at the same surface from the same distance and point of view, constrained by the nature of the surface and the more or less internalised rules of depiction to be unable to imagine of our perception that it is anything other than the seeing of one particular (complex) state of affairs. Walton denies that the imaginative acts must be deliberate or under a person's control, citing dreams as the obvious counter-examples, and also many of the imaginings that make up day-dreams. This may be so. But what we are concerned with is wide-awake persons with equal vision looking at pictures, each of whom, whenever he looks at a certain picture, is supposed to imagine in exactly the same manner, as his eyes traverse the same course, each being unable to imagine differently. And this is supposed to hold across the entire range of pictures (depictions of all kinds), from those with minimal depictive content to those however great their depictive content may be. This sort of constancy and irresistibility of imaginings does not appear to hold with any other subject matter. It would be a curious fact if our imaginations were so tightly constrained in the manner Walton requires them to be in the case of depictions, but were always free elsewhere to vary from person to person and from time to time. (Budd 2008: 212).

Finally, as discussed when considering Wolfgang Iser's view in Chapter 5, it is a common intuition that the plenitude of film renders the imagination otiose: in contrast to the written word, there is nothing left for the imagination to do. That is, Iser seeks to *contrast* perception with imagination. Why should the imagination be thought constitutive of a visual experience of a representation? The point is pithily stated by Richard Wollheim who, again, contrasts the two notions, claiming that 'imagination has no necessary part to play in the perception of what is represented' (Wollheim 1986: 46). The considerations I have brought against Walton's view are not decisive. I will, however, proceed on the assumption that depictive representations do not involve the imagination simply in virtue of being depictive representations.

I have no account as to the nature of depictive representations. I shall assume that some such account is available, and that it will be true to the phenomenology of engaging with such representations. That is, at a minimum, that the experience of so engaging is a distinctively visual experience and that it is different from a face-to-face visual experience of the same subject or scene. One of these differences is that the experience of a viewer who sees a subject or scene face-to-face will be as of a confrontation with that subject or scene, and the experience of a viewer of a depictive representation will be as of a representation relation with that subject or scene. In short, I have separated the account of what it is to be a depictive representation from the issue of the role of the imagination in engaging with a depictive representation. The question is whether there is, in fact, any role left for the imagination to play.

One place the imagination has been thought to play a role is in the relation between the audience and the events depicted on the screen. There are two philosophical routes to exploring the nature of this relation. First, one might simply wonder about the relation. Let us take as our example the audience of *Sense and Sensibility*. Do they see the events going on in Barton Cottage? Do they imagine they see them? Or is there some other relation? The second route goes via cinematic narration. The audience of *Sense and Sensibility* watch discrete scenes, apparently chosen to advance the narrative thread. As we saw in the last chapter, Jerrold Levinson, following Seymour Chatman, argues that 'if there is a narration in a fiction film, if a comprehensible story is being conveyed to us, then there is an agency or intelligence we are entitled, and in fact need, to imagine as responsible for this, i.e. doing the narrating' (Levinson 1996: 146–7).

Richard Allen has argued that members of the audience suffer what he calls 'projective illusion': 'the form of illusion central to our experience of the cinema is one in which, while we know that what we are seeing is only a film, we nevertheless experience that film as a fully realized world' (Allen 1995: 4).[1] It appears that by his claim Allen means it is, for the audience, as if they are in a confrontation relation with the events in Barton Cottage. However, this is not possible on the minimal description of what it is to experience a depictive representation. I shall consider two further candidates for the relation between audience and representation. First, we imagine of our looking at the film that it is looking at the lives of the sisters. The best defence of this can be found in (Wilson 2011: 29–105). Second, we imagine of our looking at the film that it is a looking at a documentary of the lives of the sisters. This is possibly the way Jerrold Levinson ought to be interpreted (Levinson 1996). There is also a third option I shall consider briefly: that the film generates, directly and impersonally, but visually, that we imagine the lives of the sisters. This is held by Greg Currie (Currie 1995: 179–80).[2]

---

[1] It is unfair to quote this out of the context of Allen's rich exposition. Also, as pointed out by Rob Hopkins, Allen has since repudiated the idea in (Allen 1997). See (Hopkins 2008: 159).

[2] The various arguments, positions, and objections are neatly summarized by Berys Gaut in Gaut 2011: 197–224.

Objections to the first two options are readily at hand. Both seem to have unacceptable consequences. For the first, my imagining I could see the sisters would involve imagining that they could see me; that I was there at their most intimate moments and so on and so forth. For the second, my imagining I was watching a documentary of the sisters would involve imagining that they were being constantly watched by a television crew or similar. The problem with this debate is not so much whether or not the objections are decisive, but rather that the debate is so absurd that our philosophical hunch must surely be that we have got off on the wrong foot. This I take to be some support (not decisive support, as there are other possible explanations for the apparently absurdity) for separating the question of the nature of depictive representation from the question of the role of the imagination (if any) in our relation with the events on the screen. Making this separation clarifies the nature of the debate.

The first option is that the audience imagine, of their seeing the film, that it is a seeing of the events depicted. The first point to notice is that the problem concerns the relation between the audience and the events on the screen, hence is neutral as to whether those events are believed to be fictional or believed to be non-fictional; in either case, the audience would still need an act of imagination in order to place themselves in the right relation with those events.

To assess this option we need to grasp the nature of 'the distinctively visual experience' available to us when we look at a cinema screen. As I am not concerned to defend an account of depictive representation I shall make some assumptions although these are in line with the mainstream account. The locution, introduced by Richard Wollheim, is that we *see* content *in* surfaces: faced with Vermeer's *The Milkmaid*, we see a milkmaid in the canvas. This experience manifests what Richard Wollheim calls 'two foldedness': 'I am visually aware of the surface I look at, and I discern something standing out in front of, or (in certain cases) receding behind, something else' (Wollheim 1987: 46). Depictive representations that are paintings typically differ from depictive representations that are films[3] (whether still or moving) in that in painting we are usually aware

---

[3] Of course, images on the screen may not be photographic but be the result of CGI. I shall ignore this complication as CGI presents a less difficult case for me to argue. A concern to draw on intuitions about still images prevents me from adopting Noel Carroll's suggestion of substituting 'moving image' for 'film' (Carroll 2008: 32).

of the surface as a surface, however in film we are not usually aware of the
surface as a surface. That is, someone who is looking at a painting typically
believes that they are looking at a painted surface and experiences that
painted surface as a painted surface. They see the paint smeared across
the canvas. There are cases where the first (and thus the second) of these
fails; when someone is successfully duped by a trompe l'oeil. There are also
cases where the first holds and the second fails; in the case of paintings
with highly finished surfaces in which no brushstroke is detectable (for
example, Bellini's *The Doge Leonardo Loredan*). Someone who is looking
at a film typically believes they are looking at a screen on which coloured
light is projected but does not usually experience the screen as a screen
on which coloured light is projected. Typically, they experience only the
content of the film.

What, then, is the content which audiences typically see? Here we need
to distinguish fiction from non-fiction (although, as we shall see, this distinction typically does not show up in the experience of the audience).
Fiction films are typically, to adopt some useful terminology from Robert
Hopkins 'two tiered'.

Here are two obvious and widely known facts about one way films are made. First,
many films are made by a process that involves two levels of representation. Actors,
with the aid of sets, props, and perhaps some live special effects, act out the events
the film seeks to narrate. (Call those events *the story told*.) And the complex events
involving the actors, sets, props, and the like are themselves recorded photograph-
ically. (Call the events recorded *the events filmed*.) Since photographic recording
and acting (supplemented by sets, special effects, and so forth) are both forms of
representation, the film, or at least each of the sequences of which it is composed,
is thus, in origin, the representation of a representation. It is a photographic representation of a set of events, the events filmed, that themselves represent other
events, the story told. Since the latter representation clearly bears strong points of
contact with that found in theater, we may as well call it *theatrical representation*.
(That is not to assume that there aren't important differences between the two.)
Let's call movies made in this way *two-tier* films.

Second, the lower tier of representation here, the representation of the story
told by the events filmed, is often illusionistic. The events filmed represent the
story told by presenting the appearance of the latter. More precisely, someone
watching the events filmed from the point of view of the camera would have visual
and auditory experiences matching those she would have before the events in the
story themselves. Perhaps illusion, so defined, is more aspiration than reality for
many films. Certainly it is not always even aspiration: some films refuse to attempt
illusion at this level. But that it is often at least an aspiration is the only way to

make sense of the tremendous care taken, in much film making, to get the sets and costumes right, to act convincingly, and to ensure that items of studio equipment, such as sound booms, are not visible in the filmed scene. (Hopkins 2008: 149)[4]

Given that the audience experience only the content of the film, which content do they experience? Is their experience as of the events filmed or the story told? In short, is what they see in the screen: the actor playing the sister, or the sister?

Consider a depiction, X, of another depiction Y, where Y is an illusion-istic depiction of a Z. Hopkins argues that when we experience X, what we tend to see in the surface is not Y, but Z. In his example, Y is a trompe l'oeil of a ceiling of ornate plasterwork, and X is a depiction of the trompe l'oeil. Although we see X as a depiction, what we see in X is not the trompe l'oeil, but the plasterwork. He calls this 'collapsed seeing in'. If 'representational properties' are properties of what a representation represents, and 'con-figurational properties' are any other property, we can formulate a general statement of the conditions for collapsed seeing in. For some picture P depicting a representation R of some scene Sc:

If a subject is to see only Sc in P (that is, to see Sc in P without doing so by seeing in P: R representing Sc) he or she must not see in P any configurational properties of R. (Hopkins 2008: 151)

As with the tromp l'oeil case, so with film. Spectators will typically experi-ence collapsed seeing in; they will 'see only Sc in P'; that is, they will see the sister rather than the actor playing the sister.

Audiences do this while believing that what they are seeing is an actor; they believe they are watching a fiction film in which the sister is played by an actor. Furthermore, the question is about the depicted content of the film; I am not reverting to the claim that the experience of the audience is as of a confrontation with a sister. It is also possible that the audience are able, if so inclined, to see the actor as the actor. If they were not able to do this they could not experience the quality of the acting (as Hopkins points out). Finally, I have only been talking about how an audience 'typically'

---

[4] This paper has greatly clarified my thoughts on this matter, and I have borrowed much of my discussion from it (although clearly Hopkins bears no responsibility for the use I am making of his thoughts). Hopkins argument is spelled out at greater length than mine, with useful caveats.

experience a film. Films in which the events filmed are not a theatrical representation will not exhibit collapsed seeing in.

In typical cases, therefore, the audience will see a representation of the story told. As I have put aside Walton's analysis of depictive representation, the audiences will have access to the story told without recourse to the imagination. They simply look at the cinema screen and the narrative is there to be seen. There is nothing to explain; nothing is gained by saying that we imagine of our seeing the film that we are seeing the real world— with collapsed seeing in we get that for free. We are watching a film narrative, we believe we are watching a film narrative, but typically we see the story told. Nothing is gained with the additional claim that we imagine, of the film, that it is a watching of the real world.

Even if we do not require the imagination in typical cases, what of cases in which there is no collapsed seeing in—cases in which the audience is aware of the configurational properties of the representation as configurational properties? That is, the audience is aware not of a sister in her everyday clothes but of Kate Winslet in costume. The imagination is not required here either; the audience is seeing the events filmed as what they are—the events filmed. Hence, whether or not there is collapsed seeing in, there is no role for the imagination.

It might be thought that the audience's engagement with non-fiction films parallels their engagement with fiction films that do not exhibit collapsed seeing in. That is, they see a representation of the events filmed. In some cases this is true; however, this is not typically the case. Consider a sequence in a documentary of a boat landing and the presenter of the documentary disembarking. The audience see a representation of a continuous sequence of events. However, anybody with any experience of film-making knows (indeed, any reflective member of the audience knows) that this is not a representation of the events filmed. Assuming only one camera crew, it is probable that sequences were filmed with the presenter on the boat, the boat docked, and the camera crew disembarked. The boat then docked again, and the presenter was filmed getting out. This would then all have been cut together along with some shots of the boat travelling through the water filmed at a different time, possibly a different day, and possibly a different boat. Noel Carroll pushes the point further:

Many documentaries freely use stock footage. Images of naval artillery barrages from the Normandy invasion can be interpolated into documentaries about the

Okinawa invasion. Shots of Hitler speaking produced on one occasion can be used to represent Hitler speaking at another point in his career. This is not occasional practice. It happens all the time. (Carroll 2000: 227)

Once again, the audience experiences collapsed seeing in. They do not see the events filmed, they see the story told. [5] The difference is that, believing they are watching a documentary, the content ends up in their structures of belief. It is the responsibility of the makers of documentaries to ensure that those beliefs are correct.

   Having examined the claim that we imagine of our looking at *Sense and Sensibility* that it is looking at the lives of the sisters, let us now examine the claim that we imagine of our looking at the film that it is a looking at a documentary of the lives of the sisters. There are two possible motivations for this argument. The first is to take it to be a way of delivering the mental state characteristic of fiction. What is 'less problematic' about documentaries is that they assert propositions which we subsequently believe. Imagining of the fiction that it is a documentary is equivalent to treating it *as if* it is a documentary: it is *as if* there are assertions and *as if* we form beliefs. The 'as if' beliefs are 'make-beliefs'; that is, propositional imaginings.[6] However, this is merely the familiar and flawed argument that the mechanisms for understanding fictional narratives are different from those used to understand non-fictional narratives. This is not the case; understanding a narrative is a matter of working out the content of the narrative from its surface structure. In working it out, we form a mental model and either already believe, or go on to believe, those propositions in the model which are true *simpliciter*. The second way of interpreting the argument is as claiming that fiction cannot be understood as fiction, it can only be understood as documentary. That is, there is something blocking understanding if we take a narrative to be fiction which vanishes when we take the narrative to be documentary. However, it is not clear what this block could be. It cannot be that if we think of a film under the concept fiction it appears artful and constructed and if we think of it under the concept documentary it does not, as documentaries are every bit as artful and

---

   [5] Of course, some films do not aim to leave the audience with the impression of a tidy sequence of events. However, the imagination is not needed for these either; it is only more difficult to construct the mental model.
   [6] Currie seems to hold this view. He contrasts documentary films with non-documentary films, in that the former 'consist substantially of filmic parts that support an asserted narrative...' (Currie 1999).

constructed as fictions. Our understanding of a narrative does not change if we shift from thinking of it as a fiction to thinking of it as a documentary.

I have argued that as film typically delivers collapsed seeing in, then, assuming that depictive representation is not analysed in terms of the imagination, what is represented is (in Hopkins terms) the story told. There is no role for the imagination: we do not need to imagine of our seeing the film that it is a seeing of the story told, nor imagine that it is a documentary of the story told. The two options I have considered are not vitiated because of their implausible consequences but rather because they have no substance. They are attempting to do a job when there is no job to be done.

The third option has been put forward by Gregory Currie.

What I imagine while watching a movie concerns the events in fiction it presents, not any perceptual relations between myself and those events. My imagining is not that I see the characters and the events of the movie; it is simply that I imagine that these events *occur*—the same sort of impersonal imagining I engage in when I read a novel. (Currie 1995: 179)

Currie gives up on the claim that the viewer needs to imagine him or herself to be in some relation to the events represented on the screen. His belief that the viewer does 'imagine that these events occur' is based on his commitment for other, and as we have seen flawed, reasons for thinking that imagination is the mental state peculiar to fiction. This is the option that is closest to my view; we simply see a representation of the story told, and form our mental model on the basis of that.

I conclude, then, that the imagination is not needed to mark the distinction between non-fiction film and fiction film, and is it is not needed to explain the perceptual relation between the viewer and the events depicted on screen. I have not gone into detail about what goes on in the head of the viewer of a film, although, whatever does will be very different to what goes on in the head of the reader of a book. It is time to enter a caveat. Nothing I have said so far implies that it is *impossible* for a viewer to exercise their imagination. I have agreed with Walton that the concept of the imagination needs to be clarified, and have been trying to argue that there is no good reason for thinking that imagination plays an essential role in our engagement with film. However, there are more secure uses of the term in which all sides can agree that imagination has a role. When watching a film we can imagine what it would be like to live in Barton Cottage, to face the kinds of lack of opportunities faced by educated women in Regency England, to be married to Colonel Brandon, to make love to Marianne Dashwood. We can use our imaginations to make connections: to work—for example—through the similarities and differences between Willoughby and Edward Ferrars. Furthermore, the imagination might be used in specific mental activities such as empathizing (if indeed we do empathize with fictional characters and if the mental state characteristic of empathy really is the imagination). All this I can happily allow, but it does not lie at the heart of the viewer's engagement with film.

My project, in this book, has been to argue that the imagination cannot bear the weight that has been placed on it by contemporary philosophers of fiction, and that a consequence of this is that what are usually taken to be problems to do with fiction are actually problems to do with narrative. In that sense, I hope that my 'debunking make-believe' will have the salutary effect of closing down the blind alleys, and getting us back on the road.

Bibliography

Abell, C. and K. Bantinaki (eds.) (2010). *Philosophical Perspectives on Depiction*. Oxford, Oxford University Press.

Allen, R. (1995). *Projecting Illusion*. Cambridge, Cambridge University Press.

Allen, R. (1997). 'Looking at Motion Pictures'. *Film Theory and Philosophy*. R. Allen and M. Smith. Oxford, Oxford University Press: 76–94.

Austen, J. (1975). *Sense and Sensibility*. London, The Folio Society.

Ayer, A. J. (1971). *Language, Truth and Logic*. Harmondsworth, Penguin.

Bedford, S. (1989). *Jigsaw*. London, Hamish Hamilton.

Bedford, S. (1993). *Aldous Huxley: A Biography*. London, Papermac.

Blackburn, S. (1984). *Spreading the Word*. Oxford, Oxford University Press.

Booth, W. (1991). *The Rhetoric of Fiction*. Harmondsworth, Penguin.

Bortolussi, M. and P. Dixon (2003). *Psychonarratology*. Cambridge, Cambridge University Press.

Bourne, C. and Caddick Bourne, E. (2016). *Time in Fiction*. Oxford, Oxford University Press.

Bower, G. H., J. B. Black, et al. (1979). 'Scripts in Memory for Text'. *Cognitive Psychology* 11: 177–220.

Bronte, E. (1963). *Wuthering Heights*. London, J.M. Dent and Sons.

Brooks, L. R. (1967). 'The Suppression of Visualization by Reading'. *The Quarterly Journal of Experimental Psychology* 19(4): 289–99.

Budd, M. (1985). *Music and the Emotions*. London, Routledge and Kegan Paul.

Budd, M. (2008). 'Postscript to "On Looking At a Picture"'. *Aesthetic Essays*. Oxford, Oxford University Press: 208–15.

Byrne, A. (1993). 'Truth in Fiction: The Story Continued'. *Australasian Journal of Philosophy* 71(1): 24–35.

Carroll, L. (2010). *Alice's Adventures in Wonderland and Through the Looking Glass*. New York, Cosimo.

Carroll, N. (1990). *The Philosophy of Horror*. New York and London, Routledge.

Carroll, N. (1997). 'Fiction, Non-Fiction, and the Film of Presumptive Assertion: A Conceptual Analysis'. *Engaging the Moving Image*. New Haven, Yale University Press: 193–224.

Carroll, N. (2000). 'On the Narrative Connection'. *Beyond Aesthetics: Philosophical Essays*. Cambridge, Cambridge University Press: 118–33.

Carroll, N. (2000). 'Photographic Traces and Documentary Films'. *Engaging the Moving Image*. New Haven, Yale University Press: 225–33.

Carroll, N. (2000). 'The Wheel of Virtue: Art, Literature, and Moral Knowledge'. *Art in Three Dimensions*. Oxford, Oxford University Press: 201–34.

Carroll, N. (2003). 'Art and Mood: Preliminary Notes and Conjectures'. *The Monist* 86(4): 521–55.

Carroll, N. (2006). 'Introduction to "Film Narrative/Narration"'. *Philosophy of Film and Motion Pictures*. N. Carroll and J. Choi (eds). Oxford, Blackwell: 175–84.

Carroll, N. (2008). *The Philosophy of Moving Pictures*. Oxford, Blackwell.

Chalmers, D. J. (2002). 'Does Conceivability Entail Possibility?' *Conceivability and Possibility*. T. Gendler and J. Hawthorne (eds.). Oxford, Oxford University Press: 145–200.

Chandler, R. (1955). *The Little Sister*. Harmondsworth, Penguin.

Chatman, S. (1990). *Coming to Terms: The Rhetoric of Narrative in Fiction and Film*. Ithaca, Cornell University Press.

Choi, J. (2003). 'Fits and Startles: Cognitivism Revisited'. *The Journal of Aesthetics and Art Criticism* 61(2): 149–57.

Coplan, A. (2010). 'Film and Non-Cognitive Affect'. *Film and Philosophy*. H. Carel and G. Tuck (eds.). London, Palgrave Macmillan.

Crane, T. (2001). 'Intentional Objects'. *Ratio XIV*: 336–49.

Currie, G. (1990). *The Nature of Fiction*. Cambridge, Cambridge University Press.

Currie, G. (1995). *Image and Mind: Film, Philosophy and Cognitive Science*. Cambridge, Cambridge University Press.

Currie, G. (1999). 'Visible Traces: Documentary and the Contents of Photographs'. *Philosophy of Film and Motion Pictures*. N. Carroll and J. Choi (eds.). Oxford, Blackwell: 141–53.

Currie, G. (2010). *Narratives and Narrators: A Philosophy of Stories*. Oxford, Oxford University Press.

Currie, G. and I. Ravenscroft (2002). *Recreative Minds*. Oxford, Oxford University Press.

Davies, D. (2007). *Aesthetics and Literature*. London, Continuum.

Davies, D. (2010). 'Eluding Wilsons "Elusive Narrators"'. *Philosophical Studies* 147(3): 387–94.

Fleming, P. (1964). *Brazilian Adventure*. London, Jonathan Cape.

Forbes, G. (2006). *Attitude Problems: An Essay on Linguistic Intensionality*. Oxford, Clarendon Press.

Foreman, A. (1999). *Georgiana: Duchess of Devonshire*. London, HarperCollins.

Forgas, J. P. and G. H. Bower (1987). 'Mood Effects on Person-Perception Judgements'. *Journal of Personality and Social Psychology* 53(1): 53–60.

Friend, S. (2006). 'Narrating the Truth (More or Less)'. *Knowing Art: Essays in Aesthetics and Epistemology*. M. Kieran and Dominic McIver Lopes (eds.). Dordrecht, Springer: 35–50.

Friend, S. (2014). 'Believing in Stories'. *Aesthetics and the Sciences of the Mind*. Greg Currie, Matthew Kieran, Aaron Meskin, and Jon Robson (eds.). Oxford, Oxford University Press: 227–48.

Friend, S. (2008). 'Imagining Fact and Fiction'. *New Waves in Aesthetics*. K. Thomson-Jones and K. Stock (eds.). Basingstoke, Palgrave Macmillan: 150–69.

Friend, S. (2011). 'Fiction and Imagination II'. *Supplementary Proceedings of the Aristotelian Society LXXXV*: 163–80.

Friend, S. (2012). 'Fiction as a Genre'. *Proceedings of the Aristotelian Society CXII*(2): 179–209.

Gaut, B. (2011). *A Philosophy of Cinematic Art*. Cambridge, Cambridge University Press.

Gendler, T. S. (2000). 'The Puzzle of Imaginative Resistance'. *The Journal of Philosophy XCVII*(2): 55–81.

Gendler, T. S. (2006). 'Imaginative Resistance Revisited'. *The Architecture of the Imagination: New Essays on Pretence, Possibility and Fiction*. S. Nichols (ed.). Oxford, Oxford University Press: 149–73.

Gerrig, R. J. (1993). *Experiencing Narrative Worlds: On the Psychological Activities of Reading*. Boulder, Westview Press.

Gerrig, R. J. and D. A. Prentice (1991). 'The Representation of Fictional Information'. *Psychological Science 2*(5): 336–40.

Gibson, J. (2011). 'Thick Narratives'. *Narrative, Emotion, and Insight*. J. Gibson and N. Carroll (eds.). Philadelphia, Pennsylvania State University Press: 69–91.

Gilbert, D. T. (1991). 'How Mental Systems Believe'. *American Psychologist 46*(2): 107–19.

Goldie, P. (2000). *The Emotions*. Oxford, Clarendon Press.

Goldie, P. (2012). *The Mess Inside: Narrative, Emotion, & the Mind*. Oxford, Oxford University Press.

Graesser, A. C., K. K. Millis, et al. (1997). 'Discourse Comprehension'. *Annual Review of Psychology 48*: 163–89.

Graesser, A. C., M. Singer, et al. (1994). 'Constructing Inferences During Narrative Text Comprehension'. *Psychological Review 101*(3): 371–95.

Grahame, K. (1971). *The Wind in the Willows*. London, Methuen.

Greenspan, P. (1988). *Emotions and Reasons*. New York and London, Routledge.

Hills, A. (2009). 'Moral Testimony and Moral Epistemology'. *Ethics 120*: 94–127.

Holmes, R. (1996). *Wellington: The Iron Duke*. London, HarperCollins.

Hopkins, R. (2007). 'What is Wrong With Moral Testimony?' *Philosophical and Phenomenological Research LXXIV*(3): 611–34.

Hopkins, R. (2008). 'What Do We See in Film?' *The Journal of Aesthetics and Art Criticism 66*(2): 149–59.

Hopkirk, P. (1990). *The Great Game*. Oxford, Oxford University Press.

Hume, D. (1993). Of Tragedy. *Selected Essays*. S. Copley and A. Edgar (eds). Oxford, World's Classics: 126–33.

Iser, W. (1978). *The Implied Reader: Patterns of Communication in Prose Fiction from Bunyan to Beckett*. Baltimore, Johns Hopkins University Press.

John, E. (1998). 'Reading Fiction and Conceptual Knowledge: Philosophical Thought in Literary Context'. *Journal of Aesthetics and Art Criticism* 56(4): 331–48.

Johnson-Laird, P. (1983). *Mental Models*. Cambridge, Mass., Harvard University Press.

Johnson, M. K. (1988). 'Reality Monitoring: An Experimental Phenomenological Approach'. *Journal of Experimental Psychology: General* 117(4): 390–4.

Kania, A. (2005). 'Against the Ubiquity of Fictional Narrators'. *Journal of Aesthetics and Art Criticism* 63: 47–54.

Lamarque, P. (1981). 'How Can We Fear and Pity Fictions?' *Aesthetics and the Philosophy of Art: The Analytic Tradition*. P. Lamarque and S. H. Olsen (eds.). Oxford, Blackwell: 328–36.

Lamarque, P. (2010). 'Literature and Truth'. *A Companion to the Philosophy of Literature*. G. L. Hagberg and W. Jost (eds.). Oxford, Wiley-Blackwell: 367–84.

Lamarque, P. and S. H. Olsen (1994). *Truth, Fiction and Literature*. Oxford, Clarendon Press.

Lamarque, P. and S. H. Olsen (2004). Introduction to Part VI. *Aesthetics and the Philosophy of Art: The Analytic Tradition*. Oxford, Blackwell: 295–9.

Lardner, R. (1946). *The Portable Ring Lardner*. New York, The Viking Press.

Lawrence, T. E. (1939). *The Seven Pillars of Wisdom*. London, Jonathan Cape.

Leslie, A. (1994). 'Pretending and Believing: Issues in the Theory of ToMM'. *Cognition* 50: 211–38.

Levinson, J. (1992). 'Intention and Interpretation in Literature'. *The Pleasures of Aesthetics*. Ithaca and London, Cornell University Press: 175–213.

Levinson, J. (1996). 'Film Music and Narrative Agency'. *Contemplating Art: Essays in Aesthetics*. Oxford, Oxford University Press: 143–83.

Levinson, J. (1997). 'Emotion in Response to Art'. *Emotion and the Arts*. M. Hjort and S. Laver. Oxford, Oxford University Press: 20–34.

Levinson, J. (1997). 'Emotion in Response to Art'. *Contemplating Art: Essays in Aesthetics*. Oxford, Oxford University Press: 38–55.

Lewis, D. (1978). 'Truth in Fiction'. *Philosophical Papers Vol. 1*. Oxford, Oxford University Press: 261–80.

Lyons, W. (1980). *The Emotions*. Cambridge, Cambridge University Press.

Magliano, J. P., R. A. Zwaan, et al. (1999). 'The Intermediate Effect: Interaction Between Prior Knowledge and Text Structure'. *The Construction of Mental Representations During Reading*. H. van Oostendorp and S. R. Goldman (eds.). Mahwah, NJ, Lawrence Erlbaum Associates: 151–168.

Magliano, J. P., R. A. Zwaan, et al. (1999). 'The Role of Situational Continuity in Narrative Understanding'. *The Construction of Mental Representations During Reading*. H. van Oostendorp and S. R. Goldman (eds.). Mahwah, NJ, Lawrence Erlbaum Associates.

Marsh, E. J., M. L. Meade, et al. (2003). 'Learning Facts from Fiction'. *Journal of Memory and Language* 49: 519–36.

Matravers, D. (1997). 'The Paradox of Fiction: The Report versus the Perceptual Model'. *Emotion and the Arts*. M. Hjort and S. Laver (eds.). Oxford, Oxford University Press: 78–92.

Matravers, D. (1998). *Art and Emotion*. Oxford, Oxford University Press.

Matravers, D. (2003). 'Fictional Assent and the (so-called) Puzzle of Imaginative Resistance'. *Imagination, Philosophy and the Arts*. M. Kieran and D. M. Lopes (eds.). London, Routledge.

McKoon, G. and R. Ratcliff (1992). 'Inference During Reading'. *Psychological Review* 99(3): 440–66.

Meskin, A. and J. M. Weinberg (2006). 'Imagine That!' *Contemporary Discussions in Aesthetics and the Philosophy of Art*. M. Kieran (ed.). Oxford, Blackwell: 222–35.

Morton, F. (2006). *A Nervous Splendour: Vienna 1888-1889*. London, Folio.

Neill, A. (1991). 'Fear, Fiction and Make-Believe'. *The Journal of Aesthetics and Art Criticism* 49(1): 47–56.

Neill, A. (1993). 'Fiction and the Emotions'. *Arguing About Art: Contemporary Philosophical Debates*. A. Neill and A. Ridley (eds.). London, Routledge: 250–66.

Nichols, S. (2004). 'Imagining and Believing: The Promise of a Single Code'. *The Journal of Aesthetics and Art Criticism* 62(2): 129–139.

Nichols, S., ed. (2006). *The Architecture of the Imagination: New Essays on Pretence, Possibility, and Fiction*. Oxford, Clarendon Press.

Nichols, S. (2006). 'Imaginative Blocks and Possibility: An Essay in Modal Psychology'. *The Architecture of the Imagination: New Essays on Pretence, Possibility and Fiction*. S. Nichols (ed.). Oxford, Oxford University Press: 237–55.

Owens, J., G. H. Bower, et al. (1979). 'The "Soap Opera" Effect in Story Recall'. *Memory and Cognition* 7(3): 185–91.

Pashler, H. and J. C. Johnston (1998). 'Attentional Limitations in Dual-task Performance'. *Attention*. H. Pashler. Hove, Psychology Press: 155–89.

Potts, G. R., M. F. St. John, et al. (1989). 'Incorporating New Information into Existing World Knowledge'. *Cognitive Psychology* 21: 303–33.

Prentice, D. A. and R. J. Gerrig (1999). 'Exploring the Boundary between Fiction and Reality'. *Dual Process Theories in Social Psychology*. S. Chaiken and Y. Trope (eds.). London, The Guilford Press: 529–46.

Quine, W. v. O. (1960). *Word and Object*. Cambridge, Mass., MIT Press.

Radford, C. (1975). 'How Can we be Moved by the Fate of Anna Karenina?' *Arguing About Art*. A. Neill and A. Ridley (eds.). London, Routledge: 239–49.

Radford, C. (1977). 'Tears and Fiction'. *Philosophy* 52(200): 208–13.

Rinck, M. and U. Weber (2003). 'Who When Where: An Experimental Test of the Event-Indexing Model'. *Memory & Cognition* 31(8): 1284–92.

Sainsbury, R. M. (2010). *Fiction and Fictionalism*. London, Routledge.

Schank, R. C. and T. R. Berman (2002). 'Narrative Impact: Social and Cognitive Foundations'. *Narrative Impact: Social and Cognitive Foundations*. M. C. Green, J. J. Strange and T. C. Brock (eds). Mahwah, NJ, Lawrence Erlbaum Associates: 287–314.

Schroeder, T. and C. Matheson (2006). 'Imagination and Emotion'. *The Architecture of the Imagination: New Essays on Pretence, Possibility, and Fiction*. S. Nichols (ed.). Oxford, Clarendon Press: 19–39.

Scott Fitzgerald, F. (2005). *Tender is the Night*. London, The Folio Society.

Searle, J. (1979). 'The Logical Status of Fictional Discourse'. *Expression and Meaning*. Cambridge, Cambridge University Press: 58–75.

Searle, J. (1983). *Intentionality: An Essay in the Philosophy of Mind*. Cambridge, Cambridge University Press.

Spark, M. (1961). *The Prime of Miss Jean Brodie*. Harmondsworth, Penguin.

Stock, K. (2003). 'The Tower of Goldbach and Other Impossible Tales'. *Imagination, Philosophy and the Arts*. M. Kieran and D. M. Lopes (eds.). London, Routledge: 107–24.

Stock, K. (2005). 'Resisting Imaginative Resistance'. *The Philosophical Quarterly* 51(225): 607–24.

Stock, K. (2011). 'Fiction and Imagination I'. *Supplementary Proceedings of the Aristotelian Society LXXXV*: 145–62.

van Dijk, T. A. (1999). 'Context Models in Discourse Processing'. *The Construction of Mental Representations During Reading*. H. van Oostendorp and S. R. Goldman (eds.). Mahwah, NJ, Lawrence Erlbaum Associates: 123–48.

van Dijk, T. A. and W. Kintsch (1983). *Strategies of Discourse Comprehension*. New York, Academic Press.

Velleman, D. (2003). 'Narrative Explanation'. *Philosophical Review*(112): 1–25.

Walton, K. (1978). 'Fearing Fictions'. *Aesthetics and the Philosophy of Art: The Analytic Tradition*. P. Lamarque and S. H. Olsen (eds.). Oxford, Blackwell: 307–19.

Walton, K. (1984). 'Transparent Pictures: On the Nature of Photographic Realism'. *Marvellous Images: On Values and the Arts*. Oxford, Oxford University Press: 79–116.

Walton, K. (1990). *Mimesis as Make-Believe*. Cambridge, Harvard University Press.

Walton, K. (1992). 'Seeing-In and Seeing Fictionally'. *Psychoanalysis, Mind and Art: Perspectives on Richard Wollheim*. J. Hopkins and A. Savile (eds.). Oxford, Blackwell: 281–91.

Walton, K. (1994). 'Morals in Fiction and Fictional Morality I'. *The Supplementary Proceedings of the Aristotelian Society LXVIII*: 27–50.

Walton, K. (1997). 'Spelunking, Simulation, and Slime: On Being Moved by Fiction'. *Emotion and the Arts*. M. Hjort and S. Laver (eds.). Oxford, Oxford University Press: 37–49.

Walton, K. (2006). 'On the (So-called) Puzzle of Imaginative Resistance'. *The Architecture of the Imagination: New Essays on Pretence, Possibility, and Fiction.* S. Nichols (ed.). Oxford, Oxford University Press: 137–48.

Walton, K. (2007). 'Aesthetics—What? Why? and Wherefore?' *The Journal of Aesthetics and Art Criticism* 65(2): 147–161.

Weatherson, B. (2004). 'Morality, Fiction, and Possibility'. *Philosophers' Imprint* 4(3).

Weinberg, J. M. and A. Meskin (2006). 'Puzzling over the Imagination: Philosophical Problems, Architectural Solutions'. *The Architecture of the Imagination: New Essays on Pretence, Possibiliy, and Fiction.* S. Nichols (ed.). Oxford, Oxford University Press: 175–202.

Williams, B. (1985). *Ethics and the Limits of Philosophy.* London, Fontana.

Wilson, G. M. (2011). *Seeing Fictions in Film: The Epistemology of Movies.* Oxford, Oxford University Press.

Wollheim, R. (1986). 'Imagination and Pictorial Understanding II'. *Supplementary Proceedings of the Aristotelian Society* 60: 45–60.

Wollheim, R. (1987). *Painting as an Art.* London, Thames and Hudson.

Worth, S. E. (2004). 'Narrative Understanding and Understanding Narrative'. *Contemporary Aesthetics* 2: 1–16.

Yablo, S. (2002). 'Coulda, Woulda, Shoulda'. *Conceivability and Possibility.* T. S. Gendler and J. Hawthorne (eds.). Oxford, Oxford University Press: 441–492.

Zwaan, R. A., M. C. Langston, et al. (1995). 'The Construction of Situation Models in Narrative Comprehension: An Event-Indexing Model'. *Psychological Science* 6(5): 292–7.

Index